Moodle 2.0 First Look

Discover what's new in Moodle 2.0, how the new
features work, and how it will impact you

Mary Cooch

BIRMINGHAM - MUMBAI

Moodle 2.0 First Look

First published: September 2010

Production Reference: 1170910

Published by Packt Publishing Ltd.
32 Lincoln Road
Olton
Birmingham, B27 6PA, UK.

ISBN 978-1-849511-94-0

www.packtpub.com

Cover Image by Ed Maclean (edmaclean@gmail.com)

Credits

Author
Mary Cooch

Reviewers
Alex Büchner

Susan Smith Nash

Acquisition Editor
Sarah Cullington

Development Editor
Dhiraj Chandiramani

Technical Editor
Gauri Iyer

Indexer
Tejal Daruwale

Proofreader
Lesley Harrison

Editorial Team Leader
Aanchal Kumar

Project Team Leader
Ashwin Shetty

Project Coordinator
Ashwin Shetty

Graphics
Nilesh R. Mohite

Production Coordinator
Melwyn D'sa

Cover Work
Melwyn D'sa

About the Author

Mary Cooch has been a Languages and Geography teacher in the UK for the last 25 years, Mary Cooch now spends part of her working week travelling the country as a VLE trainer specializing in Moodle. The author of Moodle 1.9 for Teaching 7-14 Year Olds `https://www.packtpub.com/beginners-guide-moodle-1-9-for-teaching-7-14-year-olds/book`, she regularly promotes its benefits in schools and has a deep understanding of what works best for younger students. She is looking forward to putting to practical use all the new features of Moodle 2.0. Known online as the moodlefairy, Mary is a moderator on the help forums of `www.moodle.org` where she aims to encourage others with her passion for this Open Source Virtual Learning Environment. Mary's blog is at `www.moodleblog.org`.

Mary is based at Our Lady's Catholic High School in Preston, Lancashire, UK, but will go anywhere to Moodle! She may be contacted at `mco@olchs.lancs.sch.uk`.

I would like to thank Packt for the chance to write another book, my family for their tolerance; Helen Foster at Moodle HQ for her behind the scenes support; Carl at CS New Media for his excellent customer service; Andrew, Stuart and Emma for (ab)use of their names and of course to my Moodle Manager Mark Greenwood for having all the Best Ideas.

About the Reviewers

Alex Büchner is the co-founder and technical lead of Synergy Learning (`www.synergy-learning.com`), the UK's and Ireland's leading Moodle and Mahara partner. He has been working with virtual learning environments of all shapes and sizes since their advent on the educational landscape. Services offered include Mahara & Moodle hosting, support, training and branding.

Alex holds a PhD in Computer Science and an MSc in Software Engineering. He has authored over 50 international publications, including Moodle Administration by Packt Publishing, and is a frequent speaker on Moodle, Mahara, and related open-source technologies.

Susan Smith Nash has been involved in the design, development, and administration of online courses and programs since the early 1990s. Her current research interests include the use of learning objects, mobile learning, leadership in e-learning organizations, and energy, and sustainability technology transfer. Her articles and columns have appeared in magazines and refereed journals. She received her Ph.D. from the University of Oklahoma in 1996, and in addition to e-learning, Nash has also been involved in international economic development training, interdisciplinary studies, international energy education (renewables and non-renewables), and sustainable business and career training. Her book, Leadership in the e-Learning Organization, was co-authored with George Henderson, and published by Charles Thomas and Sons. Her most recent books include Klub Dobrih Dejanj (Good Deeds Society) and E-Learner Survival Guide (Texture Press). Her edublog, E-Learning Queen (`www.elearningqueen.com`) has received numerous awards and recognitions.

Table of Contents

Preface

Moodle is currently the world's most popular E-learning platform. The long-awaited second version of Moodle is now available and brings with it greatly improved functionality. If you are planning to upgrade your site to Moodle 2.0 and want to be up-to-date with the latest developments, then this book is for you.

This book takes an in-depth look at all of the major new features in Moodle 2.0 and how it differs from previous Moodle versions. It highlights changes to the standard installation and explains the new features with clear screenshots, so you can quickly take full advantage of Moodle 2.0. It also assists you in upgrading your site to Moodle 2.0, and will give you the confidence to make the move up to Moodle 2.0, either as an administrator or a course teacher.

With its step-by-step introduction to the new features of Moodle 2.0, this book will leave you confident and keen to get your own courses up and running on Moodle 2.0. It will take you on a journey from basic navigation to advanced administration, looking at the changes in resource management and activity setup along the way. It will show you new ways tutors and students can control the pace of their learning and introduce you to the numerous possibilities for global sharing and collaborating now available in Moodle 2.0

This book is your personal guided tour of the new and enhanced features of Moodle 2.0

What this book covers

Chapter 1, What's New and How To Get it: This chapter gives a brief look at what Moodle 2.0 has to offer with the exciting new modules and enhanced features, and the major overhauls in the file uploading and navigation system

Chapter 2, Finding your Way Around: This chapter will cover finding our way around Moodle, with the improved navigation system and the new way blocks are dealt with.

Chapter 3, Editing Text and Adding Files: This chapter will focus on editing text and adding files – looking at the replacement HTML editor and the new way files are brought into Moodle.

Chapter 4, What's New in Add a Resource: This chapter concentrates on the "add a resource" drop-down and we investigate the different terminology and additions to this menu.

Chapter 5, What's New in Add an Activity: This chapter concentrates on the "add an activity" drop-down and we investigate improvements to existing modules such as **Quiz, Workshop**, and **Wiki**.

Chapter 6, Managing the Learning Path: This chapter deals with how to manage the learning path of our students. It focuses on **Conditional Activities** and **Completion tracking.**

Chapter 7, New Modules for Moodle 2: This chapter deals with improved communication. We'll look at the new **Comments** feature, and changes to the **Blog** and **Messaging**.

Chapter 8, Admin Issues: This looks at the admin side of things. We will go through the site administration menu, considering changes in roles, themes, filters, file uploads, and other features that don't fit in anywhere else!

What you need for this book

You should have access to an installation of Moodle 2.0, either locally hosted or online. If you plan to install Moodle, the requirements are as follows:

- PHP must be 5.2.8 or later
- One of the following databases:
    - MySQL 5.0.25 or later (InnoDB storage engine highly recommended)
    - PostgreSQL 8.3 or later
    - Oracle 10.2 or later
    - MS SQL 2005 or later

- One of the following browsers:
  - ◦ Firefox 3 or later
  - ◦ Safari 3 or later
  - ◦ Google Chrome 4 or later
  - ◦ Opera 9 or later
  - ◦ MS Internet Explorer 7 or later

If you are upgrading, you need in addition to the above you will need to have Moodle 1.9. If you have an earlier version of Moodle, you will need to upgrade to 1.9 before proceeding.

Who this book is for

If you are an existing Moodle user, tutor, or administrator, then this book is for you. You are expected to be familiar with the operation of Moodle.

Conventions

In this book, you will find a number of styles of text that distinguish between different kinds of information. Here are some examples of these styles, and an explanation of their meaning.

New terms and **important words** are shown in bold. Words that you see on the screen, in menus or dialog boxes for example, appear in the text like this: "**Choose your learning style** and **Orientation quiz** are marked complete."

 Warnings or important notes appear in a box like this.

Reader feedback

Feedback from our readers is always welcome. Let us know what you think about this book—what you liked or may have disliked. Reader feedback is important for us to develop titles that you really get the most out of.

To send us general feedback, simply send an e-mail to feedback@packtpub.com, and mention the book title via the subject of your message.

If there is a book that you need and would like to see us publish, please send us a note in the **SUGGEST A TITLE** form on www.packtpub.com or e-mail suggest@packtpub.com.

If there is a topic that you have expertise in and you are interested in either writing or contributing to a book, see our author guide on www.packtpub.com/authors.

Customer support

Now that you are the proud owner of a Packt book, we have a number of things to help you to get the most from your purchase.

Errata

Although we have taken every care to ensure the accuracy of our content, mistakes do happen. If you find a mistake in one of our books—maybe a mistake in the text or the code—we would be grateful if you would report this to us. By doing so, you can save other readers from frustration and help us improve subsequent versions of this book. If you find any errata, please report them by visiting http://www.packtpub.com/support, selecting your book, clicking on the **errata submission form** link, and entering the details of your errata. Once your errata are verified, your submission will be accepted and the errata will be uploaded on our website, or added to any list of existing errata, under the Errata section of that title. Any existing errata can be viewed by selecting your title from http://www.packtpub.com/support.

Piracy

Piracy of copyright material on the Internet is an ongoing problem across all media. At Packt, we take the protection of our copyright and licenses very seriously. If you come across any illegal copies of our works, in any form, on the Internet, please provide us with the location address or website name immediately so that we can pursue a remedy.

Please contact us at copyright@packtpub.com with a link to the suspected pirated material.

We appreciate your help in protecting our authors, and our ability to bring you valuable content.

Questions

You can contact us at questions@packtpub.com if you are having a problem with any aspect of the book, and we will do our best to address it.

1
What's New in Moodle 2

Nine years ago, in Australia, a Computer Science graduate named Martin Dougiamas was trialing a web tool he'd developed to help teachers create lessons online. Inspired by his own experiences with the outback "School of the Air". Martin's Modular Object Oriented Dynamic Learning Environment offered tutors a way to connect remotely with their students in a collaborative and supportive workspace.

Did any of us foresee back then just how global a phenomenon Moodle would become? Now used by over 31 million students in over 44 thousand sites in over 200 countries, Moodle has truly changed the face of learning.

With improved access to the internet, and with commercial companies being quick to spot a potential money-earner, many such Learning Management Systems have arisen since then. What makes Moodle special, however, is the fact that it has remained as Open Source technology. Anyone can use Moodle; everyone can make Moodle better. While official Moodle Partners will give you peace of mind if you want Moodle installed at your establishment, you are also entirely free to go for it alone. If you need advice, whether of a pedagogical or technical nature, ask in the forums at `http://moodle.org/` where the doors are never closed. If you spot an error or a bug, then someone (perhaps even you) will fix it. If you have an idea for a "plug-in" that might be useful for other Moodlers worldwide, you can put forth your suggestion to the community. The world changes constantly and Moodle changes with it.

Since its official "birth" in 2002, Moodle has gone through several full versions and a number of stable releases in between. You can even catch up on all the bug fixes and minor tweaks by downloading the weekly stable "+" build. This year, however, sees the advent of the latest, biggest, and most enhanced version: Moodle 2.0. It's a new "take" on an established package. It is rich with new features, and it retains all that was good from Moodle 1.9, blended with new ideas and improvements, suggested and developed by the huge Open Source community. Moodle 2.0 has been a long time in the making. Its arrival became somewhat of an in-joke on the forums of www.moodle.org. Over the last couple of years, the answer to many a query would has been "You can't do that yet, but you will be able to in Moodle 2.0" prompting one Moodle Partner to comment that alongside better navigation, cleaner appearance, more controlled activities, enhanced modules, and improved interaction, Moodle 2.0 was expected to "sort out wars and world famine". Well, they haven't quite managed that, (Although there's still time for Moodle 3.0!), but there are sufficient new features in Moodle 2 to warrant a close look, and that is the purpose of this book.

Why read this book?

This book aims to give users familiar with Moodle an insight into the new features of Moodle 2.0. Perhaps you've been using Moodle 1.9 as a teacher with your classes and are keen to make the most of the latest version? Or perhaps you are a Moodle admin who wants to check if you are ready to upgrade or maybe you want to ensure that you're able to help your tutors get to grips with the changeover?

This chapter will give you a few teasers of what's to come. Subsequent chapters will go into greater depth in order to prepare you for the Moodle 2.0 experience. From a learning and teaching point of view, rest assured that the object-oriented approach that makes Moodle so flexible is still solid in Moodle 2.0. In fact, there are even more ways to tailor your content to suit your learners, as we shall see in *Chapter 6, Managing the Learning Path* From an Administrator's point of view, role complexities have been tidied up, file uploads have been rationalized and Moodle 2.0 connects usefully with the best of the Open Web. While each chapter will point to new admin features where appropriate, *Chapter 8, Admin Issues* will focus on them more specifically. So what kind of thing can we expect? Let's take a tour!

Looks cleaner, moves faster

Previous versions of Moodle came with pre-installed themes, such as *Cornflower* or *Wood*, making an average Moodle site easily recognizable when meandering along the Internet. The **Downloads** tab on `http://moodle.org/` links to a **Themes** section offering an array of other contributed "skins" for Moodle to enhance its appearance. Despite this, users still complained Moodle looked "clunky" in contrast with other, commercial Learning Management Systems. In recent years, the adoption of Moodle has broadened from universities and schools to major charities, businesses, and non-governmental organizations. They want integration with their websites and a clean, professional look. Moodle 2.0 has done away with the previous themes and will ultimately include 20 brand new themes, of which **Boxxie** , as seen in the following screenshot, is one:

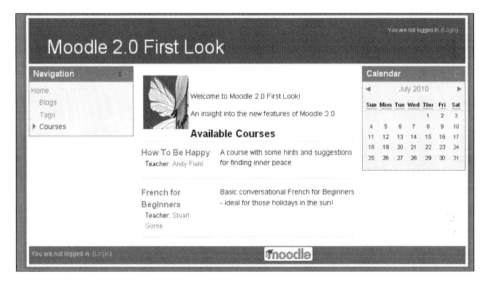

For the sake of clarity in this book, our screenshots will use the very basic **Standard** theme from now on.

In the following screenshot you'll note that the **Navigation** block on the left has been docked to the side— this is a totally new way of moving around in Moodle 2.0. We have the option of saving space and docking — or of expanding the block as with the calendar to the right:

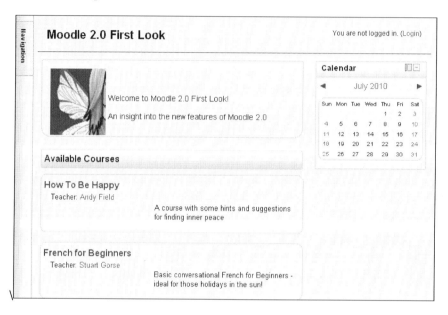

Within a course the **Navigation** block will show links to individual sections and expand to the activities in those sections. It is now possible to rename the topic sections so that these names appear in the links rather than numbered topics. If you look at the following screenshot, we are in a course **French for Beginners** and **Introduction** is actually topic 0 and **First Steps in French** is topic 1. Note also that the link at the top **My Home** takes the user straight to their **MyMoodle** page.

We'll start our tour of Moodle 2.0 in *Chapter 2, Finding your Way Around* by looking at how we navigate around the site and within a course.

A new way of managing your content

In Moodle 1.x, the **Resource** module offered the teacher in a course the ability to upload their documents, create web pages in Moodle, or even display a directory of materials. Users, who had particularly large files, say **SCORM** packages or multimedia for example, were able to upload via FTP once they knew the directory number for their course and were granted the rights to do so. Moodle 2.0 does away with most of this, using a different philosophy for file management. It has more functionality and is more secure; however, for some it might initially appear more complex to manoeuvre.

Compare and contrast the **Add a resource...** drop-down in Moodle 2.0 (on the left) and Moodle 1.9 on the right:

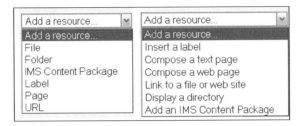

Note the simpler, clearer terms:

- **File** (instead of **link to a file or web site**)
- **Folder** (instead of **Display a directory**)
- **Page** (instead of **Compose a web page/Compose a text page**)
- **URL** (instead of **link to a file or web site**)

In *Chapter 3, Editing Text and Adding Files* and *Chapter 4, What's New in Add a Resource* we'll look more closely at the way you can display content in Moodle 2.0. While you are still able to upload all your word-processed documents and Powerpoint presentations, you can also easily embed media from other sites such as `http://www.youtube.com/` or `http://www.flickr.com/` from the new text editor (based on the popular tinyMCE editor as used in **WordPress** for example). Here's a screenshot of the so-called **File Picker** where you can see that, alongside files already in Moodle and files you might want to upload, there is a link and the facility to search YouTube:

More places to have your say

With the addition of a **Comments** facility in Moodle 2.0 it is now easier than ever for users to give feedback, voice their opinions and generally make their presence felt in your online community. A **Comments** block may be included on your course page to give the students the opportunity to rate the course or suggest improvements, as shown in the following screenshot:

We get far more control over the location and positioning of blocks in Moodle 2.0. Due to this we're not just restricted to having the **Comments** block (or others) on our course page. Most screens will allow us to add a block now, so we could for example have comments on the difficulty of **Quiz** questions, or comments on the suitability of a particular uploaded resource. The same commenting feature has also been applied to the standard Moodle blog, such that users may now, at last, comment on each others' entries.

Existing activities updated and improved

A lot of time and effort has gone into making existing Moodle modules such as the **Wiki**, **Quiz**, and, **Workshop** easier to manage and more user-friendly. The latter are two of my favorites, both very powerful yet not immediately intuitive, particularly to new users. While I found the results they gave worth the initial hours spent figuring out how to set them up, I also found that many teachers felt daunted by their complexity. As a trainer I always felt the need to apologize before I showed people how to use the **Quiz**, and I only went through the **Workshop** settings on request from advanced users. Open Source, by its nature, depends on collaboration, and several Moodle developers and enthusiasts have made significant changes to the **Quiz** and **Workshop** modules – in fact, the **Workshop** module has been virtually rewritten for Moodle 2.0, so if you shied away from it before, now is definitely the time to give it another chance. This has improved the display and the search facility of the Quiz question bank, making it not only easier to locate and reuse previously made questions but also simplifying the process needed to create a new quiz from scratch — making the Moodle Quiz a realistic option for a new user to tackle without fear of confusion.

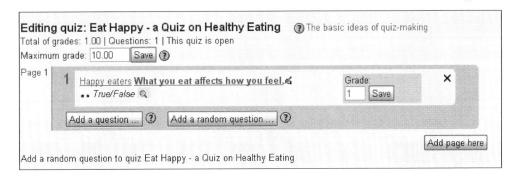

The changes to the Workshop now give us a clear view of the different stages of the assessment process:

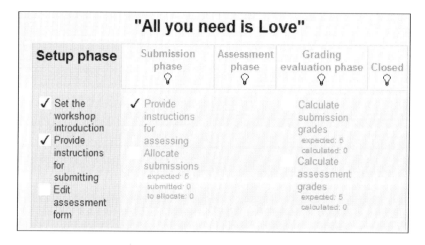

In *Chapter 5, What's New in Add an Activity* we shall set up a **Workshop** and **Quiz** in order to view their potential for our teaching. We'll also take a look at the **Wiki** which has undergone a redesign too.

Moodle has always had a **Wiki** module but with limited functionality. Some users preferred alternative wikis such as the **OUwiki** or **NWiki** instead. Indeed, http://moodle.org/ itself chose **Mediawiki** for its comprehensive and collaborative documentation. Moodler. The new, improved **wiki** for Moodle 2.0, incorporates features from **OUwiki** and **NWiki** and we'll investigate how they can enhance our students' learning experience.

Moodle's built-in **blog** feature has always been very limited, for example, offering no comment facility. Attached as it is to a user's profile meant that a student could only have one blog, rather than a number of blogs according to which course they were in. Again, for this reason, blogging Moodlers around the world looked elsewhere — such as to WordPress or to the Open University's **OUBlog**.

Moodle's **blog** is now much enhanced. If you have an external blog you can now import its posts (based on a feed URL and on tags) and use it within Moodle. You can now also associate an entry to a particular course, attach more than one file to your entry, have a proper RSS feed, and (with the **Comments** API mentioned earlier) make it possible for permitted users finally to give you their thoughts on your thoughts! In *Chapter 7, New Modules for Moodle 2* we'll consider blogs in more depth.

Another successful vehicle for the exchanging of ideas is the **Messaging** block. This block is controversial in some circles, such as in schools with younger learners, where some consider it a distraction of the MSN type while others see it as an essential means of instant communication. The messaging block has been revamped and is now event-driven, allowing users to control which messages they receive and how. We'll take a look at this too in Chapter 7 along with a quick glance at the well established **Feedback** module which is available but hidden by default in Moodle 2.0.

Control your students' progress

The word **Moodle**, although originally an acronym standing for (**Modular Object (Oriented Dynamic Learning Environment**), is also a verb. **Moodling** is the process of lazily meandering through something, doing things as it occurs to you to do them, an enjoyable tinkering that often leads to insight and creativity.

There is an irony here: with its roots in Social Constructionist Pedagogy (see `http://docs.moodle.org/en/Philosophy`), Moodle empowers students to manage their own learning: they can work at their own individual pace; collaborate with others to build on collective experiences and form new knowledge through active involvement rather than passive absorption. A Native American proverb (which has many variants) states:

Tell me and I'll forget

Show me and I may not remember

Involve me and I'll learn

And yet despite this, one of the most frequently requested features on Moodle has been a way to control the path of students' learning: *how can we set our course so a learner can only progress to level 2 once they have reached a certain grade in Level1? How can we hide the Advanced work so they can't see it until they have completed the Basic work* (in case – perish the thought – they might actually go, do the Advanced work and understand it ahead of the official schedule!)?

A workaround to controlling student access was made available for Moodle 1.9. It was known as "Activity Locking" and was a means whereby a teacher could set certain conditions on a task that the student had to meet before the next task became visible. With Moodle 2.0 this feature is standard, and is known as **Conditional Activities.** Whenever you set up an activity in your Moodle course, you now have the power to decide when to enable your student to move on.

This is essential for many situations, particularly in the commercial world. Imagine for example a Health and Safety programme where it's vital that procedures are carried out in a particular order. Or a language-learning course where students really need to understand the basics of the present tense before they can tackle the complexities of the imperfect subjunctive.

You can see the following screenshot of the setup screen of an assignment in one of our Moodle 2.0 courses. The student will not be able to tackle this assignment (indeed, not even see it) until they have made a post in an introductory forum:

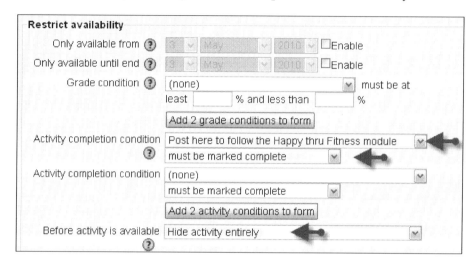

In *Chapter 6, Managing the Learning Path* we shall consider how we can best make use of **Conditional Activities,** alongside another new arrival – the ability for users to mark tasks as "done". This is the **Activity completion tracking** facility. Next to each item on your Moodle course page you will see a dotted check mark (tick). This can be either manually checked by the student if they feel they have finished a task (they can change their mind) or else the teacher can set it to be checked automatically once the student has actually completed the activity. You can see from the next screenshot that the activities **Choose your learning style** and **Orientation quiz** are marked complete. The lighter background denotes an automatic check while the grey background denotes a manual check.

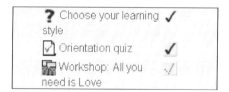

Similarly, the new **Course Completion** feature enables teachers to set conditions for a whole course or set of courses to be marked as complete – again either dependent on certain grades being obtained, activities being completed or activities being manually marked off by the students themselves.

Improved admin

Even if you're not a Moodle administrator yourself, you will notice changes in roles, groups, and other administrative features in Moodle 2.0. The Moodle developers have taken into account three types of users who would deal with admin and tried to make life simpler for them:

- The regular tutor who, besides managing students in their course, just wants to teach

- The basic Moodle admin who (like many I meet) is a non-technical teacher who's been given the job and wants to do their best, but does not have, or want, an exhaustive knowledge of every advanced feature of Moodle

- The more experienced Moodle admin who is confident working with roles

If you are a Moodle administrator you'll see that one of the most misunderstood aspects and most commonly made errors in user control has now been addressed; it is no longer possible to assign teachers or students a system-wide role. It could almost be guaranteed that on the help forums of http://moodle.org/ at least once a week you would encounter a Moodle admin confused that *all* their students and *all* their teachers appeared in *all* their courses. They had failed to read the big writing in the **Assign System roles** page of **Site Administration** and given their users global access. Now, students and teachers can only be assigned to the courses they work in and hopefully those panicked cries for help will become a thing of the past.

Likewise, admins can now see at a glance exactly which roles in which courses certain users have.

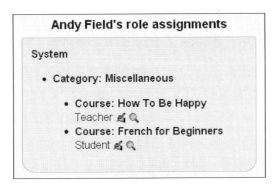

As you can see in the preceding screenshot, the user Andy Field is shown as a teacher in one course and a student in another. This makes it much easier to track users and better understand the permissions they have in different courses.

If you are a course tutor in Moodle 2.0, you will be pleased to know that yet another oft-requested feature, site-wide groups, or **Cohorts**, has been developed. This will enable the Moodle admin to create a group (class) of students that can be added, moved between, and removed from courses throughout your Moodle installation. **Cohorts** should enable us to do away with the need for metacourses or roles assigned at a category level.

System: available cohorts					
Name	Cohort ID	Description	Cohort size	Source	Edit
August Intake	AI	summer study group	3	Created manually	Edit Delete Assign

Add

We'll look at the implications of these site-wide groups along with enhanced user-management in *Chapter 8, Admin Issues*. We'll cast an overview too of other exciting aspects such as the **Portfolio API** and the **Moodle Community Hub** which promise to simplify resource sharing and make learning truly, globally collaborative.

How do we get Moodle 2.0?

The advantage of Open Source software is that anyone can grab a copy for free and have a play around with it. Of course, if you want to use Moodle for your school or business many companies will host it for you online, including Moodle's own recommended Partners.

On the main Moodle site, `http://moodle.org/`, on the **Downloads and Plugins** tab, you can access different setups of Moodle according to your requirements — from the standard packages to install on a server, to special installer packages for MacOSX and Windows if you want to try it out yourself on a local host, you will then be presented with a list of "current stable builds" to choose from. The + version is updated weekly. You can then download Moodle as either a `.tgz` or `.zip` file, as shown in the following screenshot:

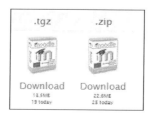

This book is intended to give a flavor of Moodle 2.0 , not to give comprehensive technical instructions for installing or upgrading. However, the following are some key points to bear in mind:

What you need for Moodle 2.0

 If you are new to Moodle admin or you want a more detailed look from an administrator's viewpoint, you might find Alex Bűchner's Moodle Administration (updated for Moodle 2.0) and also published by Packt a useful addition to your library.

It's important that either you (if you're doing this yourself) or your Moodle admin or webhost are aware of the requirements for Moodle 2.0. It needs:

- PHP 5.2.8
- MySQL 5.0.25 or else MSSQL 2005 or else Oracle 10.2

Installing Moodle 2.0 for the first time

If you are Moodle for the first time, you can find step by step instructions in the docs on the main Moodle site here: `http://docs.moodle.org/en/Installing_Moodle` and more specifically related to Moodle 2.0 here:
`http://docs.moodle.org/en/Installing_Moodle_2.0`

Upgrading to Moodle 2.0

If you already have an installation of Moodle, you will find instructions for upgrading in the docs on the main Moodle site here `http://docs.moodle.org/en/Upgrading_to_Moodle_2.0` If you are upgrading from an earlier version of Moodle (such as 1.8) then you should upgrade to Moodle 1.9 first before going to 2.0. You must update incrementally; shortcuts – for example. updating from 1.7 directly to 2.0 -- are simply not possible. Read the docs carefully if you are planning on upgrading from very early versions such as 1.5 or 1.6.

Potential problems with upgrading

Themes

The way themes work has changed completely. While this allows for more flexible coding and templating, it does mean that if you had a customized theme it will not transfer over to Moodle 2 without some redesigning beforehand.

Third party add-ons and custom code

The same applies to third party add-ons and custom code: it is highly unlikely they will work without significant alterations.

Backup and Restore

Making courses from 1.9 or earlier restore into Moodle 2. 0 has proved very problematic and is still not entirely achievable. Although this is a priority for the Moodle developers, there is at the time of writing only a workaround involving restoring your course to a 1.9 site and then upgrading it to 2.0.

Summary

In this chapter we've taken a brief look at what Moodle 2.0 has to offer. The key points to remember are that, alongside the exciting new modules and enhanced features, the file uploading and navigation systems have undergone major overhauls, such that even as you log in and attempt to put up your first resource, you will notice big changes in the way you move around Moodle. As these changes are so significant, we'll start there in next chapter.

2
Finding our way around (Navigation and Blocks)

In this chapter we'll investigate how moving around courses, course sections, and activities has changed in Moodle 2 with the introduction of "dockable" blocks. We'll look at how a user's **My Moodle** page is now an integral part of the navigation and will take a look at changes to the navigation bar (breadcrumb trail). After that, we'll focus on the side blocks, considering the increased freedom a user has to position blocks in courses, on activity pages, or throughout the site.

Meet the cast

The site used in this book contains two courses we'll be referring to in subsequent chapters. The teachers of these courses and one of their students will assist us in discovering the new features of Moodle 2.0. Let's meet them now:

	Emma Anforth	Preston
	Martin Blackforest	Southport
	Stuart Gorse	Lancaster
	Andy Field	Ely

Emma

She is just out of high school and has signed up as a student to both courses on our Moodle. She will allow us to see the changes from a student's point of view.

Martin

He is keeping an eye on both courses with the new "Manager" role in Moodle 2.0.

Stuart

He is a teacher of the **"French for Beginners"** course and will enable us to see course navigation and management from a teacher's perspective. He is very interested in controlled progression through a course and so will feature particularly in *Chapter 6, Managing the Learning Path*

Andy

He is a teacher of the **"How to Be Happy"** course and at the same time a student in the **"French for Beginners"** course. We'll follow him as he sets up collaborative learning activities.

What does Moodle 2.0 look like?

If we take a look at our Moodle 2.0 site before we log in we will see that on the left is a block called **Navigation**:

Clicking on **Courses** will display links to the two courses we have so far on our site. (We might also have a **Site News** link here too) However, if we click the icon shown in the following screenshot, we also have the option of "docking" this over to the far left as a narrow tab.

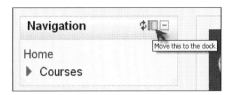

Why would we want to do that?

Because we will then have freed up space on our page and can focus on the activities in the central section. What we then get looks like this:

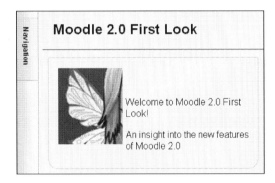

If you recall our earlier screenshot of the whole front page, it showed the **Calendar** block to the right. We can "dock" this as well, and the two blocks are neatly tucked away to one side of our screen, as shown in the following screenshot:

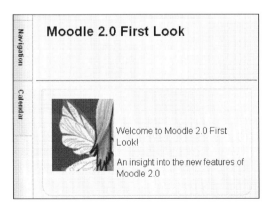

Bringing them back is easy; if we move the cursor over the docked block, it slides into view for us and we can either choose one of the links to navigate to or else to undock it. We can undock all our blocks at once by clicking the **Undock all** option at the bottom of the screen:

 This "docking" facility may be enabled or disabled for themes in **Site Administration | Appearance | Themes | Theme settings**.

What do users who are logged in see?

Let us log in and note the difference in the **Navigation** block (I've undocked it for ease of viewing).

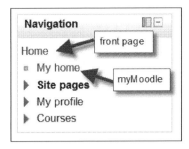

Basically there are five links here:

- **Home**: This directs us to our **front page**.
- **My home**: This takes us to our **myMoodle** page.
- **Site pages**: This is where we can access site news, items on the **front page**, blogs, and tags. Users with higher permissions can also access reports and notes from here.
- **My profile:** Here we can quickly view or edit our profile.
- **Courses**: Here we can select a course to go to.

As the **Navigation** block is a "sticky" block in all my courses (we will learn more about sticky blocks later), it means that wherever I am in Moodle I can quickly access my profile details, move to a different course, or go back to the **front page** or **myMoodle**. Let's check out these links in more detail.

Home/My home

It is possible to set the default home page for users who are logged in to **myMoodle,** instead of the **front page** in **Site administration | Appearance | Navigation**. We'll look into this in more detail in *Chapter 8, Admin Issues* when looking at admin issues. If we did that, our block would look as shown in the following screenshot:

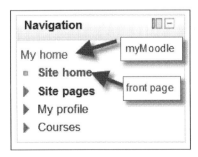

If I click on **My profile** to view my details, you can see how the navigation bar works. We can see the top bar when **Home** is our Moodle front page; and we can see the bottom bar if we're using **myMoodle** as our logged in home page:

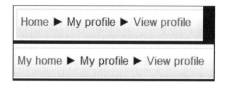

Site pages

What we see when we click on **Site pages** depends on our permissions on the site. For example; I, as the administrator with front page powers can see the view on the left as shown in the following screenshot, whereas our student Emma and her two teachers, Stuart and Andy can only see the **Blogs**, **Tags**, and **Site news** links on the right.

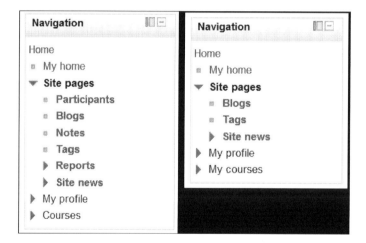

My profile

Again, note the differences between what I (as admin) see (on the left) and what regular users like our student Emma see (on the right). We'll deal with **Private files** and **Repositories**, as shown in the following screenshot, later in the book.

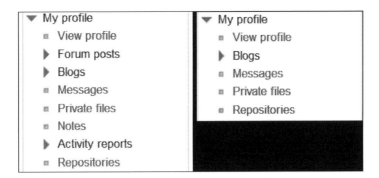

If we click the **View profile** link, our profile appears in the main screen but it also summons another block with settings for editing the profile. Emma's profile is shown in the following screenshot:

 We're going to see this often as we navigate around Moodle 2.0. Selecting a feature or activity will bring up a dedicated area in a **Settings** block enabling us to customize our choice.

My courses

We'll shortly take a look at how moving around a course has changed. This is the link to go to the courses we teach or study in.

 It is also possible from **Site Administration | Appearance | Navigation** to have all courses or course categories shown in the block along with our individual courses. This will be covered in *Chapter 8, Admin Issues*.

The Settings block

Along with the **Navigation** block, there is also a **Settings** block which becomes available once we've logged in. Like the links in the **Navigation** block, those in the **Settings** block depend on the user's permissions and roles. The following screenshot of users who are logged in on the **front page** will help explain this:

- **Emma**, our student, is only able to access her profile settings.
- **Martin**, who has been made Manager of the front page, can access settings to edit the front page as well as his profile.
- The **Admin** (me ☺) has site administration settings in addition to profile access and front page power.

As with the **Navigation** block, the arrowhead and linked words expand to show the full list of options. This makes for a much neater first view.

A good example is to compare and contrast what an administrator of a Moodle 2.0 site sees in their **Settings** block (on the left as shown in the following screenshot) with what an administrator of a Moodle 1.9 site sees (on the right, as shown in the following screenshot).

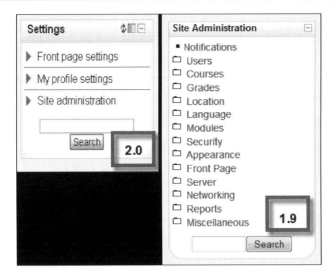

Of course, if we click that **Site administration** link in Moodle 2.0, we will see a long list of admin options, many of which are similar to the ones visible in Moodle 1.9. We'll investigate them in more detail in *Chapter 8, Admin Issues*.

Navigating around a course

That's about it for the **front page**; let's click on that **Courses** link in the **Navigation** block now and head off to Stuart's **French for Beginners** course to look at it from a teacher's perspective. When Stuart accesses his own course, this is what he sees in the **Navigation** block, as shown in the following screenshot:

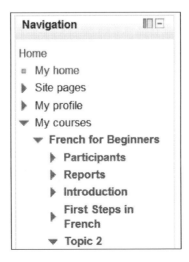

Again, as seen in the front page, he has links to the following:

- **Home**: Back to the **front page**
- **myMoodle**: Back to the **myMoodle** page
- **My profile**: It gives him profile options

What we're focusing on here, though, is **My courses**.

Stuart is a teacher in just one course, **French for Beginners**. When expanded, the list first offers us several links:

- **Participants**: An important and useful link to everyone in the course
- **Reports**: Another important and useful link to the logs and so on
- **Introduction**: This is actually **Topic 0** (and were we to expand it, we would find links to the news forum and other items Stuart has included in **Topic 0**)
- **First Steps in French**: This is actually **Topic 1** (and we will expand it in a moment to find links to items Stuart has included in **Topic 1**)
- **Topic 2**: This expands to display the list of activities in **Topic 2** and so on...

Named topic sections

A brand new and very welcome feature of Moodle 2.0 which we have just encountered is the ability to name topic sections (if your course is set to topics) and have those names reflected in the links in the navigation bar. If we do nothing, then **Topic 0** is called **General** and the other topics are displayed as numbers like **Topic 2**, but the ability to name them makes moving around much more user-friendly.

Let's take a quick look at how to name topic sections as this makes a significant difference to the appearance of our **Navigation** block. Stuart's going to name **Topic 2** so he turns on the editing in the usual way and clicks on the edit icon next to the number 2 as he normally would:

1. He unchecks the **use default section name** box.

2. He then types in his own chosen topic name as shown in the following screenshot:

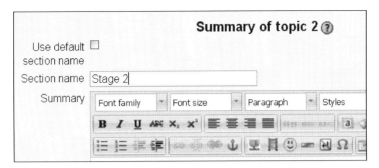

3. This ensures that this name is reflected in the link in the **Navigation** block, instead of the numbered topic:

 If the course is in weekly sections, then the weeks display in the list in a similar way to the topic numbers or names.

We can further expand the links to display the activities within those topic sections. So if, for example we click **First Steps in French** (which is the renamed **Topic 1**) we then get:

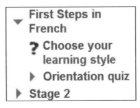

Additionally, in selecting that one particular topic in the **Navigation** block, that section becomes the only one visible in the central area of Moodle. As with Moodle 1.9, we can click on **Show all topics** or use the **Jump to...** menu to see other sections, as shown in the following screenshot:

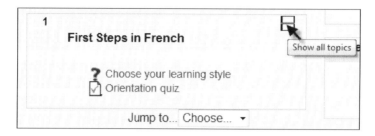

What does a student see?

Student Emma has a fairly similar view in her **Navigation** block when she goes to Stuart's French course, but with a couple of differences:

- She has a link to the other course she is studying (which of course Stuart would have if he were involved in more than one course).

- She does not have the **Reports** link that a teacher like Stuart would have.

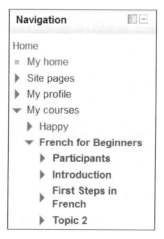

Configuring the navigation block

Logged in as admin, and with the editing turned on, if we click on the edit icon of the **Navigation** block, we are taken to a screen giving us a selection of display options, as shown in the following screenshot:

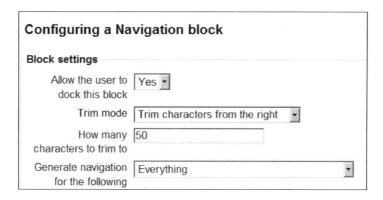

1. We can either allow or deny the user the option of docking the block

2. If the links are too long, we can choose whether to cut them off from the right or the left or centre

3. If we choose to trim the links we can choose by the number of characters

4. We can choose what we want to see in our **Navigation** block, as shown in the following screenshot:

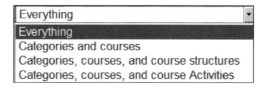

Further in the screen below are other settings we can select in the **Navigation** block that relate to its position, but we'll look at those options shortly, when we study blocks in general.

The Navigation bar (*breadcrumb trail*)

This refers to the links at the top of the screen that take you back one step at a time to other areas of Moodle. When Emma accesses the **Orientation quiz**, this is how the breadcrumb trail appears:

So she can move back to the topic (**Topic 1-First Steps in French**) or she can move back to the course itself (**French for Beginners**) or she can go back to the **front page (Home)** She can't directly, from the navigation bar, go to a different course, although she is able to do this from the **Navigation** block we've been investigating.

The course administration block

We'll look in greater detail at **Course administration** when we consider site administration as a whole in *Chapter 8, Admin Issues*. However, for now, it's useful to note that our student Emma, will still have a limited view in this block as she did in Moodle 1.9 (her grades) but that our teacher Stuart has more options than she had previously:

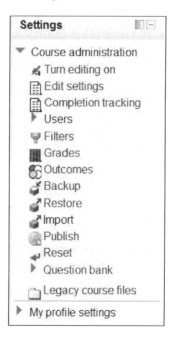

Very briefly, what's new is:

- **Completion tracking**: If this is enabled, Stuart can set checks next to each activity so students can monitor their progress. This will be discussed in detail in *Chapter 6, Managing the Learning Path*

- **Users**: This replaces the 1.9 **Assign roles** and is where Stuart or other teachers would enroll students, put them into groups, and check their permissions. This will be discussed in detail in *Chapter 8, Admin Issues*

- **Filters**: It's now possible to have filters (such as multimedia filters/text filters, and so on) enabled or disabled in individual courses rather than globally for everyone. This will be discussed in detail in *Chapter 8, Admin Issues*

- **Publish**: With Moodle's new **Community Hub** a teacher can elect to share or *publish* their course so others may benefit from it. This will be discussed in detail in *Chapter 8, Admin Issues*

What admin sees

Note that under his **Course administration** settings, Stuart sees his profile setting and the option to switch roles. If I were in the course, as admin, I would also have the **Site administration** link.

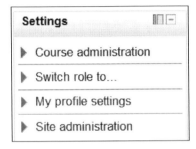

It's time now to take a more general look at blocks in Moodle 2.0 and how to manage them.

Managing blocks

Moodle has a great number of useful blocks that may be added to the front page, an individual course or made "sticky". In Moodle 1.9, it was also possible to add blocks to certain activities and resources if the administrator enabled this setting. Blocks are a very neat way of displaying information. The standard blocks include an **online users** block, an **RSS feed** block, and a **random glossary entry** block. Many more contributed blocks are available from the **Downloads and Plugins** tab of http://moodle.org/ New to Moodle 2.0 are the **Comments block**, the **Private Files block**, the **Community block,** and the **Completion block**, all of which we'll investigate later on in the book.

So, what's so different about them in Moodle 2.0. We need to first realize that blocks can be placed on pretty much any page in Moodle and that any block can be made "sticky".

 The option in 1.9 **Site Administration | Modules | Blocks | Sticky blocks** no longer exists in Moodle 2.0.

Let's test out the new blocks system by adding blocks in different regions of Moodle:

- A site-wide "sticky" block
- A block in course category pages
- A block in all areas of one particular course

Making a block sticky throughout our Moodle

Let's remind ourselves of what our front page looks like; it should look as shown in the following screenshot:

We see that there is a handy calendar on the right. A Moodle calendar will display site-wide dates of importance, events, and deadlines for classes or groups and can, of course, serve as a handy memory-jogger for individual users. This would be a valuable block to have everywhere on our Moodle site, so how do we go about achieving that and making the calendar block "sticky"?

We need to be admin on Moodle, as only the administrator can make blocks "sticky" everywhere. If we want to have an instance of the calendar block everywhere we need to head for one of the administration pages that are available from the **Site administration** link. We will add the calendar block to one of those pages and then make it sticky from there:

1. Go to the **Notifications** page (for example) and turn on the **blocks editing** on the top right

2. Select **Calendar** from the **add a block** drop-down menu

3. Click on the **configuration** icon (usually a hand/pen), as shown in the following screenshot:

4. This will bring up the following screen:

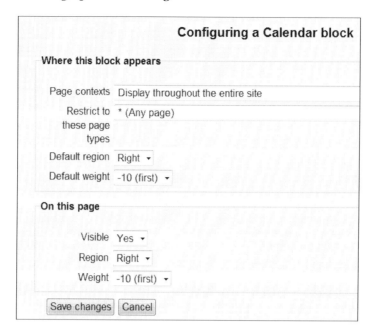

The **Page contexts** drop-down shows the following:

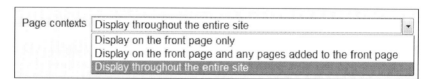

We're obviously choosing to **Display throughout the entire site**.

The **Restrict to these page types** drop-down list shows the following:

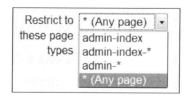

The asterisk * is a "wild card" character that represents any instances of that page. So if we select admin *, then the block will appear on any page with **admin** in the url (such as the **Browse list of users** page) However, if we choose the asterisk * (Any page), the block will then appear on all pages of our Moodle.

Default region allows us to choose whether the block will appear on the right or the left and **weighting** offers us a number to determine its position (importance) on the page where **-10** is at above all other blocks and **+10** is underneath all other blocks. If two blocks happen to have the same weighting, then the order is effectively random.

On this page gives us the choice of customizing how we want the block to appear on the page we are currently viewing - or indeed, if we don't want it to appear at all, by choosing **visible (no)**!

Note that (as we saw when clicking on **View Profile**) now we've opted to edit the **Calendar** block, we can perform extra actions in the **Settings** block:

These **Permissions** options would formerly have been available to us as tabs; they're now links in a section of the **Settings** block.

If we save the settings for our **Calendar** block and then go back to Stuart's French course, we see he's now got a useful **Calendar** block on the top right of his course page:

One important aspect to note in the preceding screenshot is that, although our teacher Stuart has editing permissions to hide, configure, or move the calendar, he does not have the usual delete icon (**X**) because it was made "sticky" by the administrator. If he clicks on the configure (pen/hand) icon all he can do is alter the calendar's visibility, location, and weighting on this actual page.

 In the preceding example, we already had an instance of the **Calendar** block on our front page. Once we made the **Calendar** block "sticky" we will have two calendars on the front page, so we would need to go and delete the first one. This is something to bear in mind when an administrator adds a block site-wide that might already be present in a course or on the front page.

Adding a block to a course category page

Suppose we would like to make an information block on the page that lists our courses in the **Miscellaneous** category? We want to put general information there about the courses, but we don't want it cluttering up the courses themselves; nor do we need it in any other category pages? Note that you'd need appropriate permissions to edit this page; a regular teacher wouldn't be able to add to a course category page.

To achieve this, we start at our **Miscellaneous course** category page, which for us is:

`http://www........./ course/category.php?id=1`

1. Turn on the editing on the `...course/category/php?id=1` (or whichever) page, and choose HTML from the add a block drop-down menu.

2. Click the configuration (hand/pen) icon.

3. Add information to the HTML editor in the normal way you would for any HTML block.

4. In the settings that follow, choose the options shown in the next screenshot:

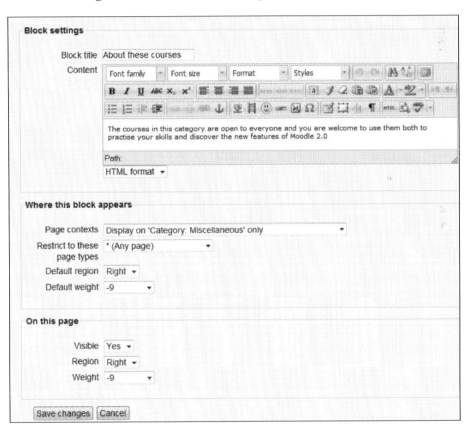

5. **Page contexts**: Here you can choose whether to display this information block on the category page or on other related pages (the course pages).

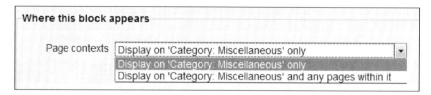

6. **Restrict to these page types**: Choose precisely which sections you wish the information block to appear on.

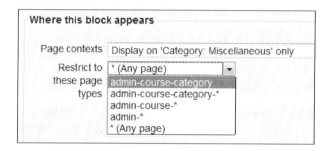

7. **Default region/weight**: Decide yourself which side (right or left) you want the block to be displayed and in which order of importance. Our calendar is 10; so it will currently display top right; if this block is 9; it will be directly beneath the calendar.

8. Save the changes.

A user, logged in or not, coming to this page now will see this extra information block. The following screenshot shows our student Emma's view. Once she goes into a course, however, because of the way we set it up, the block is no longer there.

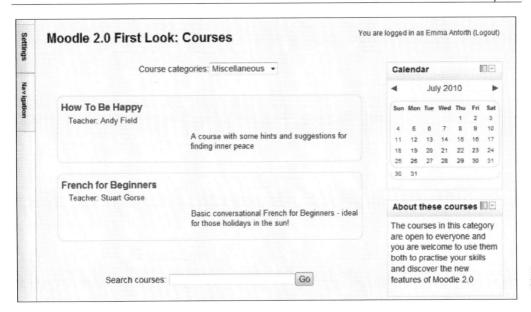

Adding a block to courses in one category

We just saw how as admin or with appropriate permissions, we can add a block to a single course category page. We also saw as we did so that we had the option of adding the block to the courses themselves as well.

When and why might we want to do this? If it is a useful and relevant block for all courses in a category, then adding the block this way will save individual course teachers having to create the block themselves and will also create consistency across the category. One such block is the new **Comments** block.

The **Comments** block (which we'll study in greater depth in *Chapter 7, New Modules for Moodle 2*) allows users to make comments on courses, resources, and activities throughout Moodle. It would be useful for both Andy and Stuart as teachers to have a **Comments** block in order to get feedback from their students.

To achieve this, and assuming we have appropriate permissions, we need to start on the course category page again:

1. With the editing turned on, the ...course/category/php?id=1 (or whichever) page and choose **Comments** from the **Add a block** drop-down menu.

2. Click the configuration (hand/pen) icon.

3. In the settings below, choose the options as shown in the next screenshot:

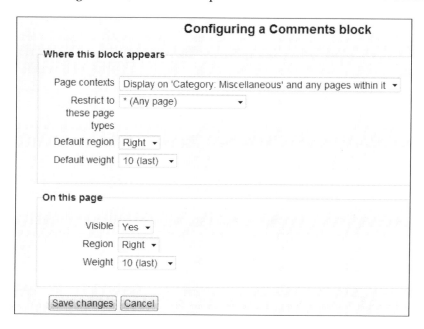

What we've done is set up a category block which will appear everywhere in that category because we have set:

- **Page contexts** to **Display on 'Category: Miscellaneous' and any pages within it**

- **Restrict to these page types** to *(Any page)

Let us now follow Stuart back into his French course and discover what teachers can do with blocks.

Teachers managing blocks in courses

With his editing turned on, Stuart can configure, move, or hide the **Comments** block but he cannot delete it as it was set up by the admin of the category.

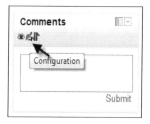

However, he can easily add (and subsequently delete) his preferred blocks to his course as teachers have always have been able to in Moodle. What is different in Moodle 2.0 is that these blocks can be displayed on all pages of the course and/or privately in the teacher's course admin pages too.

Stuart wants to set up the messaging block so that students can message each other and himself whatever activity they happen to be doing at the time. Here's how he does it:

1. With the editing turned on, select the messaging block from the **add block** drop-down menu.

2. Click the configuration (hand/pen) icon and set up the block as shown in the next screenshot:

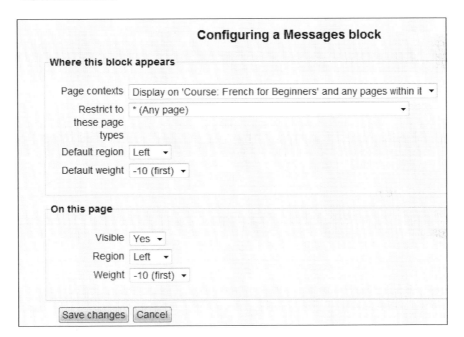

3. **Page contexts**: The drop down offered him the following options:

He chose to have the messaging block appear on all pages in the course.

4. **Restrict to these page types**: The drop-down menu offered him the following options:

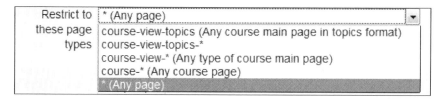

Stuart selected ***(Any page)** so the messaging block appear will appear on all screens of his course.

5. **Default region/weight**: This is set to **Left/-10** and the block will therefore appear top left.

We can check this out by following student Emma into the **Orientation quiz** where we see she has the ability to send messages as she is working on it:

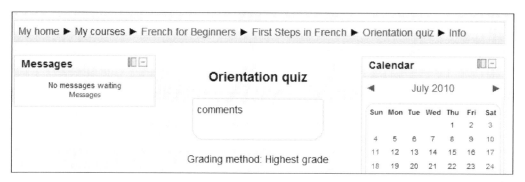

Is it a good idea to allow her to message her friends as she does the quiz? Probably not! So to finish off, let's check how teachers in courses such as Stuart can hide and move blocks around.

Hiding blocks

With his editing turned on, Stuart can navigate to the **Orientation quiz** (through the link in the **Navigation** block as we saw before or simply from the central area of the course page). He then accesses the messaging block in the quiz. He has two options:

- Hide the messaging block with the "eye" in the usual, pre-Moodle 2.0 way
- Click the edit icon and set the block to be unseen on this page

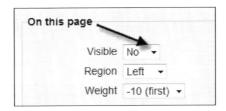

What he shouldn't do, of course, is press the delete (**X**) icon, because that would delete his messaging block from the whole course.

Moving blocks

Stuart wishes to move the **Comments** block so it is above the calendar. As with hiding, he has two options:

- Click the edit icon and reset the default region/weight to the desired position
- Click the move icon and move the block manually

The move (up/down arrow) icon is familiar with earlier versions of Moodle. If you had Ajax enabled in your site you might have had a different icon like a handlebar, for moving resources and activities. However, even though we don't have the Ajax handlebar icon for our block, we'll still see the presence of Ajax when Stuart moves his block. In the following screenshot, from left to right:

1. The block to be moved is selected.
2. Colored bars with dashed lines appear throughout the page. Clicking into the bar where block is to be moved.
3. The block has been moved.

If we were to click on the configuration (hand/pen) icon of the **Comments** block now, we'd see that its default weight for this particular page has now changed to **-10**, making it the top one on this side.

Summary

In this chapter, we began to find our way around Moodle 2. We saw that:

- Navigation around and within courses has been improved by the addition of a **Navigation** block which can be docked to one side until we need it and a **Settings** block which includes some features of the former **Administration** block but with more functionality

- Topic sections can be named and either these names or the relevant weeks appear in the **Navigation** block

- The navigation bar (breadcrumb trail) is more clearly laid out and can either default back to the front page or myMoodle according to your wish

- Blocks can be managed in a much more precise way, both by the admin when making "sticky" or category wide blocks and by teachers when they are managing them within courses

Now that we can find our way around, in *Chapter 3, Editing Text and Adding Files* we'll navigate to a course, edit some text, and upload some resources: the next major new features we'll be investigating in Moodle 2.0.

3
Editing Text and Managing Files

In this chapter, we'll begin to set up a course. We'll provide descriptions for the materials using the new HTML editor and will look at uploading and accessing resources with the enhanced file management system. We'll discover that Moodle 2.0 gives us a private file storage facility and we shall also investigate how our students can export work they've uploaded to Moodle to an external portfolio such as **Google Docs** or **Mahara**.

Typing and editing text in Moodle 2.0

Whenever we want to add text in Moodle, we click on the editing icon. It often resembles a pen and hand, but varies according to your chosen theme. This takes us to a screen we can type into. The textbox we type into is known as the HTML editor, although for most of the part we just compose our sentences; change the font styles, colors, and sizes in a WYSIWYG way. A few of the icons in the toolbar of this HTML editor are similar to the ones we might use in regular Word processing programs such as MS Word or Open Office.

In Moodle 2.0, the HTML editor has been replaced with a version known as Tiny MCE, a very popular Open Source editor you might have encountered in content management systems or blogging software such as WordPress. Along with Internet Explorer and Firefox, it will work with web browsers such as Safari, Chrome, and Opera, unlike Moodle's previous HTML editor. The following screenshot shows the new editor (on the bottom) with the original editor (on the top):

Let's take a brief look at what's changed in this new editor. The following screenshot highlights existing features which have new icons and new features not which were present before. Those aspects which have not been altered have been ignored:

Feature number	Description
	Find and replace words/phrases
	Toggle full screen mode
	Citations/abbreviations/acronym

Feature number	Description
	Select all
	Clean up messy code
	Remove formatting
	Paste as plain text
	Paste from MS Word
	Select text color
	Select background color
	Insert or edit image
	Add Moodle media
	Horizontal rule
	Non-breaking space character
	Insert a custom character (for example. symbol/accent)
	Insert a table
	Insert a new layer
	Edit CSS style
	Visual control characters on/off

Feature number	Description
HTML	Edit the HTML source code
	Preview what you've typed
	Toggle languages of the spellchecker

As you can see then, there are many more options available to us when adding descriptions of our materials or summaries of our courses. However, one of the most powerful new features is the ability to add and embed media directly from within this new HTML editor.

Embedding multimedia in the HTML editor

Let's click on the **add Moodle media** icon, number 12 in our preceding table, and explore what happens:

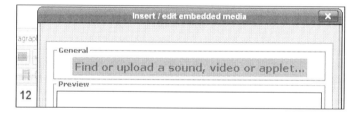

A pop up asks us to **Find or upload a sound, video or applet...**. Clicking there takes us to Moodle's **File Manager** or **File Picker** which we'll investigate in depth shortly. We can click on **Upload a file and upload a video or sound file** and it will appear automatically embedded. What's more intriguing however, is the **YouTube** option there.

We shall explore this in greater detail later and also in the final chapter where we look at administration issues, but for now it's enough for us to understand that Moodle 2.0 gives us the ability to search external sites such as YouTube and Flickr for resources that we can then very easily bring into our Moodle.

 The sites we see as an option here depend on which sites have been enabled by admin and also the context of our uploading. For example, we clicked the multimedia icon so we have a YouTube video option; had we chosen the image icon (number 11 in our table), we'd have been given a link to Flickr.

Here's an example I set up that you might like to replicate to test this out:

- I typed **Moodle Moodle Martin Dougiamas** into the **Search videos** box and a number of YouTube videos appeared for me to choose from:

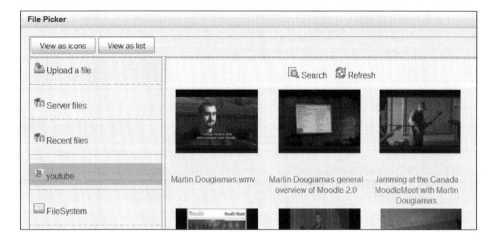

- I clicked on the one I wanted and it appeared in the box, prompting me to give it a name, add an author and suitable license, and select it for inclusion:

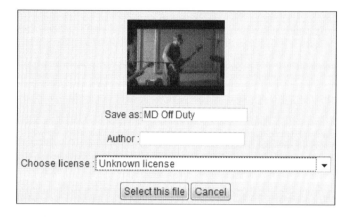

- Moodle then took me back to the popup we got when first clicking on the media icon. The YouTube movie is in the preview area, as shown in the following screenshot:

- I clicked **Insert**, saved my changes —and— voilà!

If our multimedia filters are enabled, then the video will appear automatically embedded - no need to copy and paste any code; no need to have a different tab or window open in our web browser to search YouTube—it's all done from within the new Moodle Tiny MCE editor!

Managing files

Perhaps, having just had the first sight of the files set up in Moodle 2.0, now is the time to investigate this more thoroughly and in the context of a real course. Moodle 2.0 has dramatically altered the way files are uploaded and managed. We'll begin our exploration over the next few pages and continue it (for admins) in the final chapter.

Instead of a lengthy passage on the theory behind these changes—let's just follow our Manager, Martin; our teacher, Andy; and our student, Emma as they upload resources and learn from what they do:

We don't have to upload via the **Add a Resource** dropdown; we can also upload via a link in the HTML editor—just as we could before. So, let's start by seeing how Martin adds some information to the front page.

Uploading through the HTML editor

Martin has the new "Manager" role in Moodle 2.0 He doesn't appear or participate in courses but can edit and manage them. He's a bit like the old Category admin. He's been given charge of our Moodle front page and would like to add a link to a pdf with a summary of what's new in Moodle 2.0.

>
> If you want an area on your front page to add text or images, you tick (check) the box named **add a topic section** in front page settings.

1. He turns on the editing on the front page , types text into the HTML editor, highlights the words he will link to, and clicks on the link icon, as shown in the following screenshot:

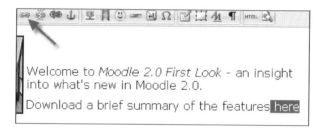

2. This brings up a popup asking him to insert a URL. However, clicking on the box to the right of the URL prompt **(1)** will take him back to the **File Picker (2)** that we met earlier:

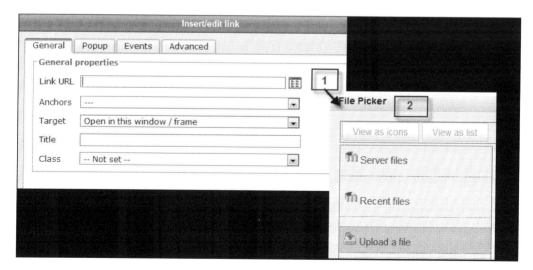

3. When Martin clicks **Upload this file...** , the browse bar we saw before appears with the extra options to name an author, set a license, and, finally, upload:

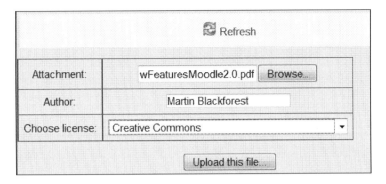

4. Moodle then goes back to the first screen where the URL box is filled with the address of the file and other options such as the target window and the link title.

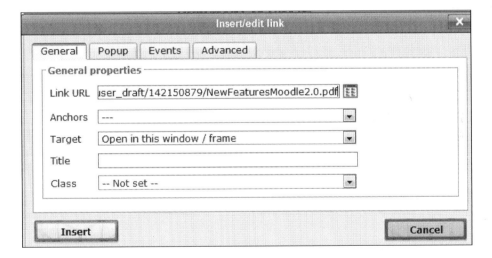

5. Clicking **Insert** will add it as a text link in the HTML editor of our front on our front page.

So what's so different about that? Although there are a few visual differences in the popup we get — and there are tabs offering more options – uploading a file using the link icon in the HTML editor doesn't seem that challenging a task. But—where exactly did it get uploaded to?

Where's our file on the front page?

Let's go back to the **File Picker** and see if we can locate that pdf which Martin just uploaded. It's here that we start to understand the differences between the New Way and the Old Way. This time we don't want the **Upload this file...** link as our pdf is already on Moodle.

If Martin clicks on **Recent files** he sees the file he's just uploaded, as shown in the following screenshot:

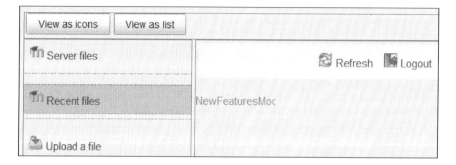

If he clicks on **Server files** he has an alternative view, as shown in the following screenshot:

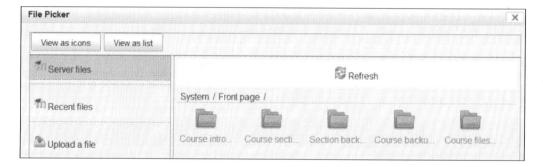

 If you don't like the icon view, you can click the **View as list** tab instead

This view is quite different from the course files of the older version. Every section on the **Front page** (or any course as we'll see) has its own dedicated folder. Our pdf was uploaded and linked to in a section summary at the very top of our Moodle front page. So we'd need to look in the **Course section summaries**.

Let's click into the folder **Course section summaries** and locate it:

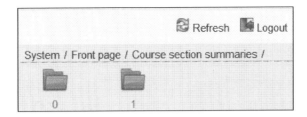

If we click into the folder numbered **1**-there is Martin's pdf!

If you recall when Martin first uploaded, he simply browsed, located, and uploaded the, paying no attention to how it should be stored in the files area. If we had done that in Moodle 1.x (as many newbies do), we'd eventually end up with huge, messy course files area crammed with a different file types designed for different topic sections of our course. If we'd been organized we might have put certain file types into folders. Our course files might have looked something like this:

Name	Size	Modified
RiverProcesses	**141KB**	17 August 2008, 03:29 PM
backupdata	**22.6MB**	17 August 2009, 03:06 PM
hotpotatoes	**9.3MB**	18 October 2008, 11:29 AM
images	**71.4KB**	3 January 2009, 03:11 PM
moddata	**840.1KB**	3 January 2009, 01:21 PM
powerpoints	**202.5KB**	9 July 2009, 07:16 PM
riverscities	**113.8KB**	18 October 2008, 01:54 PM
worksheets	**47KB**	29 October 2008, 12:32 PM

Now, however, the system for uploading has changed. Previously, an uploaded file could only be used in that one course. If we wanted it elsewhere in our Moodle, we had to upload it to another course. This often resulted in multiple instances of files—a nuisance and a drain on the server. Now, when we upload a file into one course, it is given a reference code and if we want to use it elsewhere, we just call up that code and Moodle will locate and display that file for us. All information about files and where they are used is stored in the database and the files themselves are stored on the file system. Moodle will do a check on each file to ensure identical files aren't stored twice. If we forgot we'd already uploaded a file and went to upload the file a second time, Moodle would work out, behind the scenes, that our pdf is already in the database (by doing an SHA1 , check `http://en.wikipedia.org/wiki/SHA_hash_functions`),

The **File picker** will give us the same view and path to our files wherever we are on our Moodle site. Therefore, if Martin wished, he could go to a different course, locate his pdf from the front page, and add it there as well. Let's look more closely at the path at the top when Martin clicked on **Server files**:

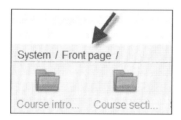

He currently sees folders with resources relating to the **Front page**, which is where he is now. Wherever we are in Moodle 2.0, the server files will default to showing us the folders for the course we are in at that moment.

If he clicks back to **System**, he will see what is shown in the following screenshot:

1. **Martin Blackforest** is his own, personal file storage folder. (We'll look at the advantages of this later on in this chapter)

2. **Miscellaneous** is the (default) category name and it houses the two courses on our Moodle site. If he clicks on it, he sees the folders relating to the **How to Be Happy** course and the **French for Beginners** course, both of which he has access to.

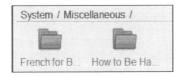

3. **Front page** is where we came from, where all the folders with **Front page** resources would be and where Martin's pdf is located.

Reusing a file in another course

Supposing Martin was in a different course and wanted to display a resource he'd uploaded elsewhere on Moodle? Previously, he'd have had to reupload it, as every course has its own separate course files area. Now, he can follow the path in the **File picker** to retrieve his file. Here's an example:

Martin is in the **How to Be Happy** course where Andy is a teacher. He'd like to display the overview he put on the front page. The following screenshot shows the journey he needs to make when he accesses the **File picker**:

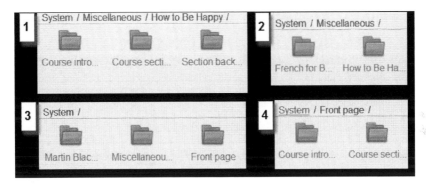

1. This is the **current course** view. It's the default view when accessing **Server files**. Here, it's the **How to Be Happy** course where Martin is working just now.

2. This is the **category view** showing available courses. We just have the **Miscellaneous** category. (Note that Martin doesn't have to click here ; he can click straight into **3**)

3. This is the **System view** which makes available the **Front page** folder.

4. This is inside the **Front page**. The **Course** section summaries hold Martin's pdf as we saw earlier.

Martin would then select his file and save into the new course.

Uploading a file from the Resource menu

Let's now follow our teacher Andy to the **How To Be Happy** course and upload an MS PowerPoint presentation (Of course our students would need to have the correct software or an appropriate viewer to see it, but that's not the remit of this book).

1. With the editing turned on, Andy as usual selects the **Add a resource** drop-down menu. Unlike we saw in Chapter 1, it looks slightly different now:

2. He selects **File** – a simpler and more obvious a choice than what we had previously, which was **link to a file or website**.

3. In the editing screen with the (now familiar) HTML editor Andy can write a description.

4. To upload the file, he clicks on **Add...**, as shown in the following screenshot:

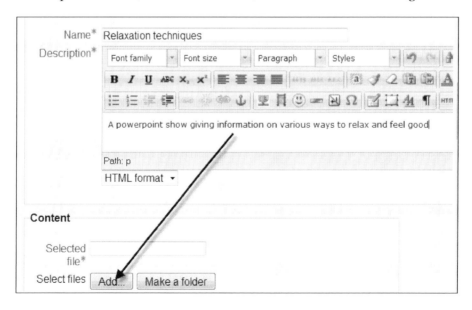

5. Clicking on **Upload this file… in the File picker**, he then browses for, locates, and uploads his presentation:

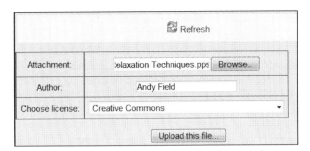

6. His file now appears, as shown in the following screenshot:

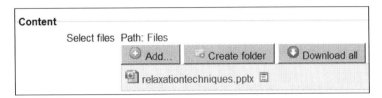

There are a few options in **Advanced Settings** we may wish to decide upon and which are not too dissimilar from older versions of Moodle:

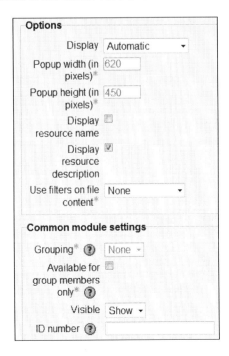

1. Clicking **Save and Return to course** makes Andy's presentation appear on the course page as we'd expect.

So, just to get this new file systems clear in our minds, lets see if we can find it again:

Where's our file in the course?

Back in the File manager, Andy selects **Recent files** and can see his presentation immediately:

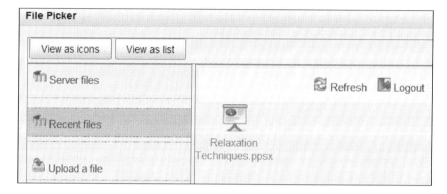

If he selects **Server files** he sees the following:

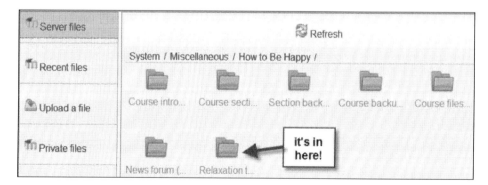

We can see the folder which must contain his PowerPoint and if he clicks on it, he sees the following screenshot:

Alongside a folder that would store the backup, and a folder containing the description, is the folder where his actual PowerPoint resides:

Follow the path!

Note the path we follow: we go from **System** to **Miscellaneous** (our course category) to the actual course and its contained resources. Perhaps the following screenshot, which starts in the category view, might make it clearer:

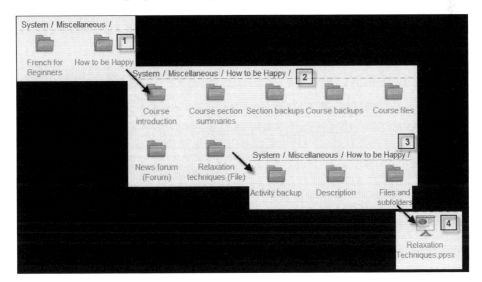

 Of course, you can also upload whole folders to Moodle instead of individual files. We shall see how to do this when we explore in greater depth the **Add a resource** drop-down menu in *Chapter 4, What's New in Add a Resource*.

What about "Course files"?

Regular users of Moodle 1.9 such as course tutors are used to the familiar "course files" structure as found via the link in the course administration block. It reminds them of the view they have on their own computers or network. This New Way of uploading might well cause some confusion for people. At the time of writing, the developers and Moodle community are discussing ways to ease this transition. Users in Moodle 2.0 have a **Private files** section which can be configured to have a folder structure that might also serve as a reassuring storage area. The Moodle admin can also enable a **Course files repository** in **Site administration** | **plugins** | **repositories** | **manage repositories**. A teacher may add files to the **Course files** link at the bottom of their course administration settings as before and find them in the file picker. The steps to do this are as follows:

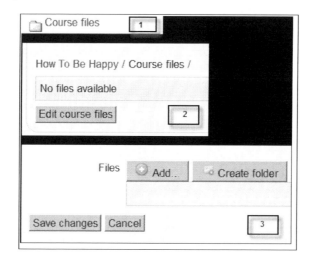

1. Andy clicks the **Course files** link.

2. He clicks **Edit course files**.

3. He may then click **Add...** to be taken to the file picker to upload a file or create a folder to create and edit a folder of his choice.

If Andy wants to locate his file again or reuse it in the same course, his file will now be more easily accessible. He can either click the same **Course files** link as he just did (**1**, in the following screenshot) or else access the course files repository from within the file picker (**2**, in the following screenshot)

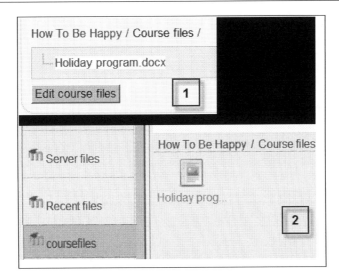

What about FTP?

Likewise, if you have very large files and are used to uploading them via FTP into the appropriate numbered course files folder, you might also be somewhat concerned if there is no longer such a place in the `moodledata` directory. We'll look at workarounds for this in *Chapter 8, Admin Issues* when we study the administration side of Moodle 2.0. Along with our Google Docs, YouTube, Flickr, and other repositories, there is one available called **File system**, and it is a fairly simple matter of creating a folder on your server, uploading there via FTP and adding it as the File System repository. That way, when users get to the **File Picker** they will have a link directly to the folder on the server with any FTP'd files. Alternatively, for those who are familiar with its advantages in Moodle 1.9, it's possible to enable a `Webdav` repository and use that.

Importing an image from Flickr

Students will benefit also from the new features of the **File Picker**. They will be able to access any repositories the Moodle admin that their teacher provides for them. On the **How To Be Happy course**, Emma is contributing to a forum where she's asked to share with others a photo of her own which makes her feel good. She can, of course, upload a photo from her computer as an attachment in the traditional way, but if her photos are stored online she can access them directly from the **File Picker**.

Emma has a photo on her personal Flickr site that she wants to use in her forum post. She can get to Flickr in the File Picker and display her image in two ways, as shown in the following screenshot:

- She can click the image icon in the HTML editor (**1**)
- She can click **Add...** under the forum post (**2**)

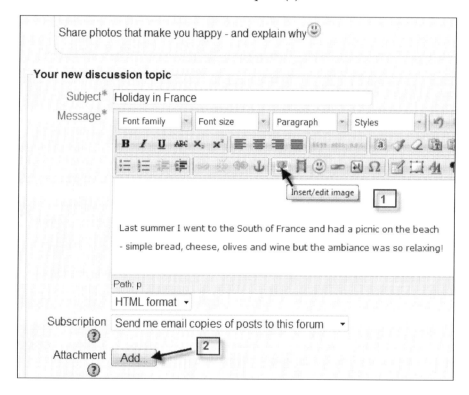

In the **File Picker** (providing her admin or teacher has enabled it) she has a link to Flickr and is prompted to log in to her account:

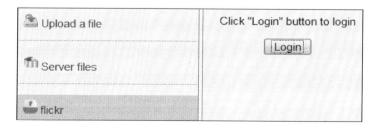

Once logged in, she can select the image she wants to import into her forum post:

She will then be prompted to save it to Moodle. If she wishes, clicking on **external** will keep the link back to the original file on Flickr rather than bringing into Moodle.

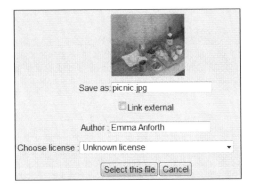

If she used the image icon in the HTML editor to locate her photo, (rather than the **Add** button) Emma will be able to define its alignment, proportions, spacing, and border in the **Appearance** tab

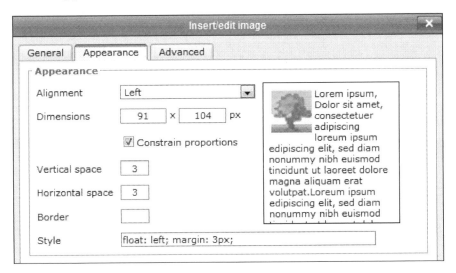

Her forum post now looks as shown in the following screenshot:

Using images from other Flickr users

What if Emma doesn't have a Flickr account? Along with the **Flickr repository** Emma used above, there is also the **Flickr public repository** which allows users to search throughout Flickr (as we did on YouTube). Again, it needs to be enabled by an admin, but if it is, then we see a link in the **File picker** allowing us to locate an image (1 below) and make our choice (2 below)

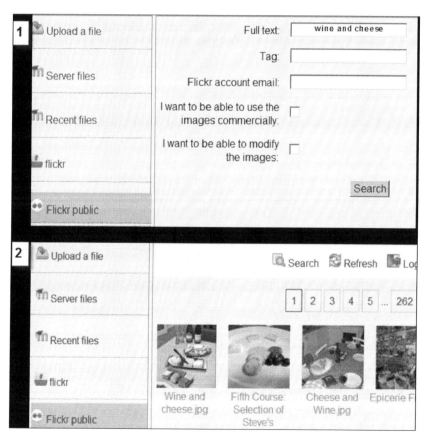

Private files – personal storage space

As mentioned before, everyone on our Moodle has a folder with their name which is used for private storage. Moodle 2.0 has a new block: **My private files.** If it's enabled in a course, it's a quick way to access that individual storage space. This is a great new feature. Various add-ons or workarounds have been available for this in the past, but this is now standard in Moodle and offers great potential. For example, tutors and students can upload a file in the office, company, or school and download it at home to continue working on it. Teachers who liked the old **course files** link can create a similar structure in their private files area to store resources and select from there those they wish to display to their students.

All users have the same view of the block:

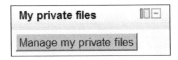

Let's take a look at student Emma's private files view.

- **Manage my private files** is what she clicks on to reach her files and this is what she sees next:

- Clicking **Add** will take her to the **File Picker**, where she sees a link to her private files, but of course there's nothing in there!

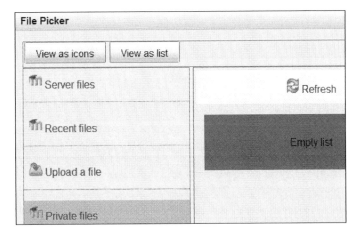

- If she clicks **Upload a file,** the resource will be uploaded into her **Private files** as the shown in the following screenshot:

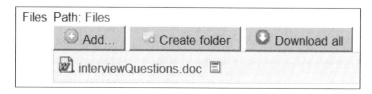

Note the little box to the right of the resource name. Clicking on it gives her a number of options, as shown in the following screenshot:

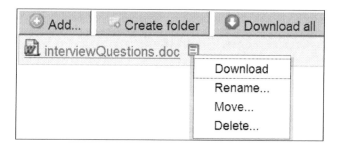

Note that now she has uploaded something, we've acquired another tab:

- **Download all** gives her the option of downloading the contents as a zipped folder

- **Create folder** enables her to create a folder for her files thus:

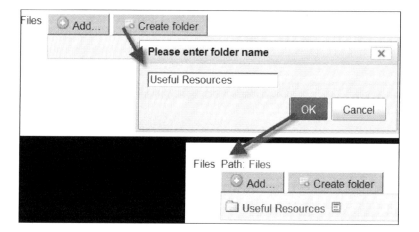

Clicking **Add...** then will upload resources directly into that folder
(See the navigation links at the top in the next screenshot)

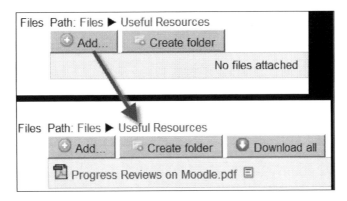

- When saved, this folder will appear in Emma's **My private files** block for
easy access:

Sending work out of Moodle with the Portfolio API

We've been looking at getting files into Moodle. Now let's get them out! It's time to
consider another useful new feature: the **Portfolio API**

Moodle 2.0 enables you to have content captured and "pushed" to external
repositories – in other words, you can send work from Moodle to another site such
as the Open Source e-portfolio site Mahara or to Google Docs. This is very useful
for students as they can build up their own e-portfolio of work that has been first
handed in to their teacher and graded on Moodle. If exported to Mahara for instance,
they can add it to a **View** (a Mahara webpage) and share with other students or
tutors for the purposes of peer review and feedback.

Let's go back to our student, Emma, and see how the process works:

Exporting an assignment

Emma has been set an assignment to upload a pdf of a slideshow she is to present next week. Note that she could have saved a draft version of this in her **Private Files**, worked some more on it, and then uploaded it via her link in the **File picker**.

The following screenshot shows her uploaded assignment:

To the right of her uploaded file, we see an icon which, when clicked on, will take us to an external repository such as Google Docs. If there is more than one repository enabled, then she will have to select the one she wants. When Emma chooses Google Docs for the first time, she gets a message requesting access to her Google Docs account:

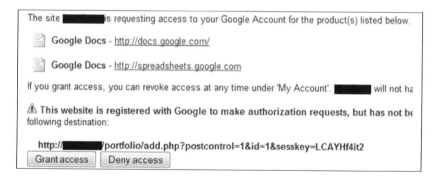

When she clicks **Grant access,** Moodle will then "push" her pdf to Google Docs, with the following success message:

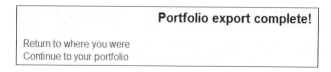

Exporting a forum post

In a similar way, it's possible to export a forum post. Emma has written a post about **The Day My Dream Came True**. Alongside the regular forum options, she can now click **Save** to send her post elsewhere:

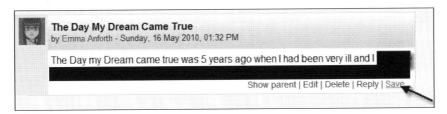

In this instance, she saves to Google Docs once more. If she clicks **Continue to your portfolio**, we can see both items in her Google Docs account:

 In order for the portfolio API to work it has to be enabled by the site admin and the desired repositories selected. We shall look at how to do this in the final chapter where we focus on Moodle admin.

Summary

In this chapter, we've investigated the way text and files are handled in Moodle 2.0

- We've seen that there is a new text (HTML editor) based on the popular TinyMCE editor, and we have looked at how it differs from the HTML editor in previous versions of Moodle

- We've seen how the opportunities to embed multimedia are greater and simpler with this new editor

- We have taken a look at how to upload files and where they are stored, contrasting the system with that of Moodle 1.9

- We've also discovered that Moodle 2.0 offers the possibility of sourcing and displaying content from other sites such as Flickr or Picasa

- We've investigated the opportunity to use the **Private files** option for personal storage

- We ended our journey into the text and files domain by considering the potential given to our users by the **Portfolio API** which allows users to push selected pieces of work directly to other sites such as Mahara or Google Docs

Having taken a brief look into these first two chapters of navigation, text editing and file upload, it's now time to look in more depth at what is new and improved in each of the dropdown menus once we have our editing turned on. *Chapter 4, Editing Text and Adding Files* will focus on the **Add a Resource** menu.

4
What's new in Add a Resource

In this chapter, we will take a look at the drop-down menu, **Add a resource**, which appears on our course pages when we have the editing turned on. We will investigate how it has changed in Moodle 2.0

New look – new wording

Let's compare the former view of the **Add a Resource** drop-down menu with the new one. In the following screenshot, the left side shows us the Moodle 2.0 view and the right shows us the Moodle 1.9 view:

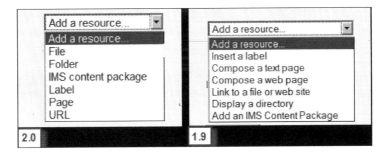

The first thing to notice is that the wording is simpler –no more confusion amongst teachers as to what constitutes a *web page* as opposed to a *text page*; no more explanation needed that **Display a directory** actually just means *Show a* **folder** *of my resources*.

The developers of Moodle 2.0 have taken onboard comments made by trainers and frequent users that certain terms were misunderstood by beginners. In the past, I myself have had to reassure newbies that even though they think they know nothing about web design, it is safe to select **Compose a web page** because doing so will simply bring up a text box where you can type your information or instructions straight into Moodle. Similarly, not everyone understands that a *directory* is just a fancy name for a folder that can house a number of your resources. This has now been made clearer. The selection **Link to a file or web site** has also been altered as these are now dealt with in two different ways. Let's take each option one at a time and study it in more depth.

Adding a file

The link **File** replaces the Moodle 1.9 **Link to a file or web site** option and is the place where, within your course, you would ordinarily upload and display files such as a Microsoft PowerPoint slideshow or a PDF resource. Selecting this from the drop-down gives us the editing screen, the top part of which is shown in the following screenshot:

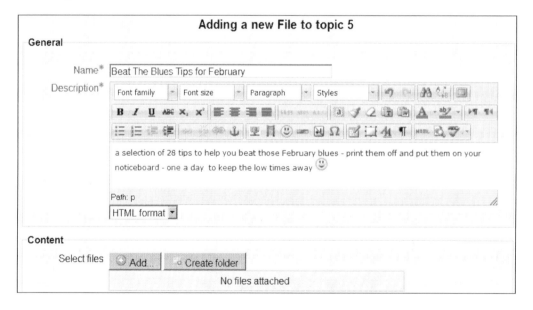

In our **How to Be Happy** course, our teacher, Andy, is going to upload an Open Office (odt) file with a tip a day for staying cheerful in February, a somewhat grim month in the Northern Hemisphere. Here's how we do it:

- For **Name**, as in earlier versions of Moodle, type the text you wish students to click on to access the resource.
- For **Description**, type a description which we can later decide to display or not. An Admin can set it so you aren't required to type a description.
- Click **Add** to start uploading the document – the **File Picker** appears:

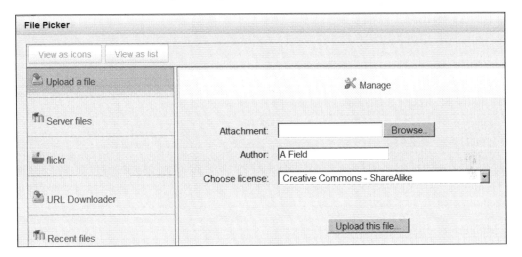

- If it's not offered by default, click **Upload this file...**
- Add the author name and license type (as we saw earlier in this book)
- Then, as with Moodle 19, click **Browse...** to locate the document and then **Upload this file...** to upload it.
- You'll be returned to the main editing screen where the document appears as a blue link.

As we scroll down, and with **Advanced** set to *Show,* we see other settings, some new, and some familiar from previous versions of Moodle but with extra functionality:

- **Display**: Choose how you want the file to appear and if you want the actual file name and/or its description to be shown. (More on this shortly)

- **Advanced**: With this enabled, you can decide the size of the pop up window and whether or not to filter the content

- **Common Module settings**: (as with Moodle 1.9) Decide whether to make the document visible or not and to set it for groups/groupings (which are now enabled by default)

- **Restrict availability**: This will only appear if the setting has been enabled in site administration and is a feature that lets you decide when and under what conditions the file may be accessed. (More on this in *Chapter 6, Managing the Learning Path*)

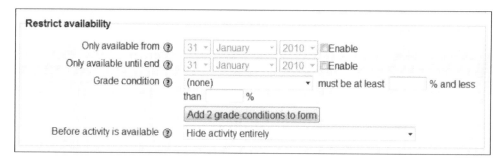

- **Activity completion**: This will only appear if you've enabled it in your course. It's a feature allowing students to check off what they have done or teachers to set activities to be automatically checked as complete under certain circumstances. (More on this in *Chapter 6, Managing the Learning Path*)

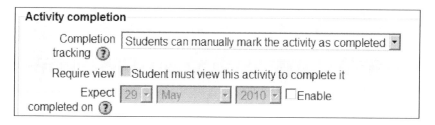

- **Save**: According to your preference, as with Moodle 1.9

Displaying a file

As we went through the settings to upload and show our February Beat The Blues tips, we noticed a drop-down option **Display**. It gives a variety of ways a file such as our .odt document can appear on the course page in Moodle 2.0. How they display will depend on their file type.

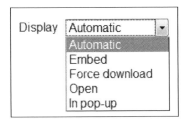

Display: **Automatic** Leave this as the default if you want Moodle to decide for you! In the case of Andy's slideshow, it's the traditional way of displaying an uploaded document, where once clicked on, it appears with a prompt box saying something like (depending on your browser) "do you want to open or save this file?"

Display: **Embed** This will show the Moodle page with heading, blocks, and footer. It will show the title/description of the item and display the file directly in the page as well, so is good for videos, flash animations and so on.

Display: **Force download** When a user clicks on the file, the web browser pops up with a "where do you want to save this file?" box.

Display: **Open** This offers no Moodle heading, blocks, footer or description; it just shows the file as it is.

Display: **In pop-up** This will cause the link to the file to appear in a pop up window before prompting you to open or download it. You can set the size of the pop up window on the **Advanced** settings page.

Site administration | **plugins** | **Activity modules** | **file** gives us two other display options if so desired. These are:

Display: **In frame** This will show the Moodle heading and the file description, with the file displayed in a resizable area below

Display: **New window** This is very much like 'in pop-up', but the new window is a full browser window, with menus and address bar, and so on

Resource administration

If we click to update our file once it has been uploaded, we can see a new area in the **Settings** block, giving us options to manage this uploaded resource. We've seen this before: when clicking to update an item, we can tweak it from here.

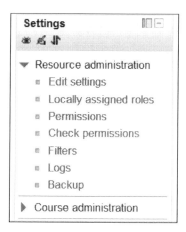

Let's take a look at these:

Edit settings

Here's where we update the details, display options, and so on (obviously!).

Locally assigned roles and Permissions

Moodle 1.9 gave us the facility to assign roles and permissions locally to an individual resource, so this is not new.

In Moodle 2.0 the site administrator has more control over who can assign which roles by default — something we'll investigate in *Chapter 8, Admin Issues*).

Check Permissions This is new however and enables to us be doubly certain our students are allowed (and not allowed!) to access what we want them to.

Let's try an example: suppose Andy hides his February tips until the end of January but that he would like one particular student, Emma, to be able to access them in advance of time. He will allow her to view the February document even though it is hidden. He needs to ensure she doesn't have the right to see any other of the hidden files until the appropriate time. Here's what to do:

- In **Locally assigned roles**, give Emma the teacher role. This will allow her to view hidden activities, and therefore, our hidden February tips.

- In **Check permissions**, select Emma and click **Show this user's permissions**.

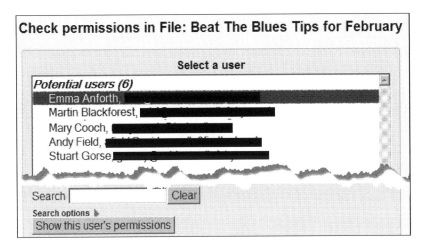

This brings up a table showing what Emma's permissions are in this file. She can view hidden activities, and therefore, would be able to see the hidden February resource in advance of the other students.

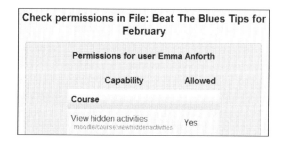

We see that because Emma's been assigned locally the role of teacher in our February document she is allowed to view the hidden file—but as she is still a student in the course as a whole, she doesn't have this right elsewhere –so we are safe!

Adding a folder

The next item in the **Add a Resource** drop-down is **Folder**, which replaces the confusingly named **Display a Directory** from earlier versions of Moodle. This is a very useful resource as it enables a number of files to be uploaded in one go, rather than individually, and it allows teachers to create a tidier looking course page by having their files showing inside a folder rather than in a long and rather tedious list. In our case, Andy is uploading a folder containing all his **Happy Hints** from 2009. Selecting the **Folder** option brings up the editing screen, the top section of which is shown in the following screenshot and which resembles that of the **File** option:

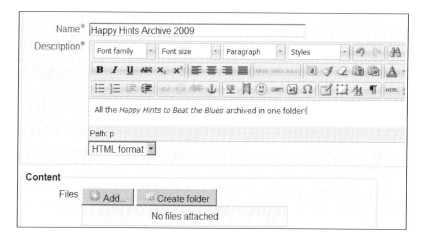

While **Name** and **Description** work in the same way as when we uploaded a file, the two options at the bottom deserve closer inspection:

Add is where we are about to click to upload our (zipped) folder to Moodle.

Create folder is where we would go to create a new folder if we wished. Clicking on it will give us the following box to enter our folder's name:

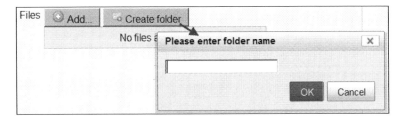

Uploading a folder to Moodle

Here's what we have to do in order to upload a whole folder rather than a single file:

- Click on **Add**. The **File Picker** appears as when we uploaded a single file
- From the **Upload this file...**, browse for and upload a resource as before. We need to upload our folder as a zipped folder, of course.

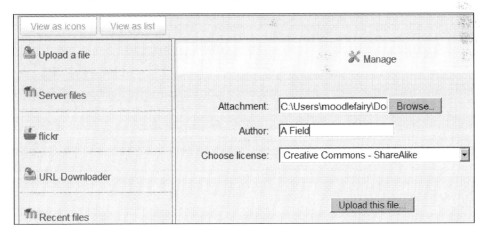

- The file link will appear in our editing screen for this resource. To the right of it is an icon -click it and it offers some choices:

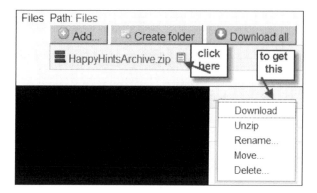

- Select the **Unzip** option
- The unzipped and zipped folders will both appear then. Click the icon again to **Delete** the zipped version if you wish.
- Note you can also **Rename** it or **Move** it to a folder you have created.

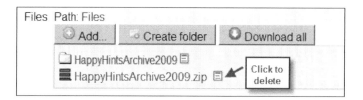

 We now have a third box that appears – the option to **Download all** the items listed below (as a zipped folder)

- Save your folder in the usual way. It appears on the course page in the way we are familiar with, and when clicked on, the files appear:

Adding an IMS content package

An **IMS Content package** is an international standard for simple learning content that is created by authoring software. It is useful if you have materials from a different LMS/VLE which you would like to reuse in Moodle. Moodle IMS CP can read it and show the content.

Previous versions of Moodle also had an option to upload an **IMS Content package** via the **Add a resource** drop-down menu, but the settings are slightly different now:

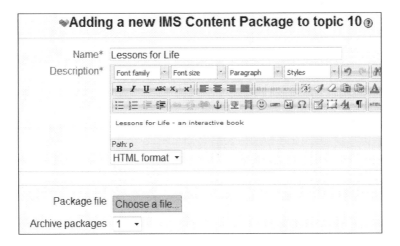

- **Name** and **Description** are entered in the usual way
- Click on **Choose a file...** to upload the IMS package
- The **File Picker** appears – from Upload a file, upload your IMS package
- It will display underneath the **Choose a file...** button.

Note its neat movable navigation bar when deployed:

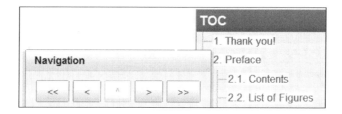

Inserting a label

A **label** is basically an empty space on a Moodle course page which can be used for breaking up long lists of resources. Its advantage is that it will hold images, sound, video, or code in addition to simple text.

Moodle has had labels for many years and in Moodle 2.0 there is not much new about them. However, the addition of the new TinyMCE HTML editor (which we looked at in *Chapter 3, Editing Text and Adding Files*) makes it easier to insert more than just words. Andy's adding a Meditation podcast in the form of an mp3 sound file to a label in his **How to Be Happy** course. It is done as follows:

- Click on **Label** from the **Add a resource** drop down
- Type in the introductory text to the mp3 file
- Type and select some blank spaces and click the link icon in the editor:

- In the pop up that appears next, click the button to browse for the file as shown in the following screenshot:

- In the **File Picker** that appears next, from **Upload this file...** browse for and upload your mp3 file

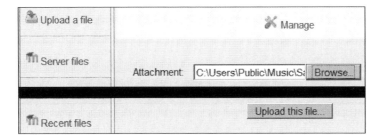

- Click **Insert** and **Save**. The label displays the mp3 in its own player for the user easily to click on and hear:

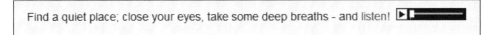

So what's new? Other options for our label

Our mp3 podcast appears in its own player because Moodle's multimedia filters are enabled. In Moodle 1.9 and earlier, this was an all or nothing feature throughout the site. However, Moodle 2.0 now allows teachers in individual courses to switch on or switch off this functionality at your own will.

If we click to update the completed label, we get a label management section in the **Settings** block above our **Course Administration**:

Clicking on **Filters** presents us with the choice to turn on or off the multimedia filters that will display (or not display) Andy's mp3 podcast. This could be useful as sometimes you might need students to download a media file rather than have it play directly from your course page.

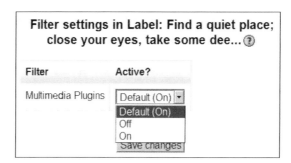

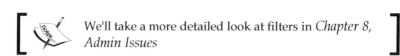 We'll take a more detailed look at filters in *Chapter 8, Admin Issues*

This same feature is available for the **Page** resource, which we'll take a look at now.

Page

Moodle 2.0's **Page** replaces the **Compose a web page** and **Compose a text page** option of earlier versions of Moodles. It is a versatile resource for displaying static content in an easy to access way: teachers prefer it because it doesn't involve going through the (often) many steps to uploading a word-processed document and students prefer it because they can get to the learning materials with one click, rather than having to open or save a file for which they might not even have the right software.

Adding a page

As with the **Label**, the new **Page** resource in Moodle 2.0 uses the enhanced TinyMCE HTML editor. Clicking on it in the drop down brings up an editing screen, the top part of which is shown in the following screenshot Andy posting directions for reaching the venue for a face to face session coming up shortly:

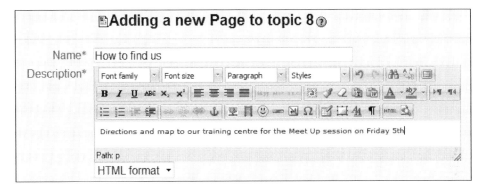

- **Name** and **Description** are entered as with other resources; whether the description is displayed or not can be decided further on.

- The drop-down box defaulting to HTML format allows us to choose either HTML or plain text when we type into the editor, similar to the former Compose a text page resource.

- Scroll down and note how the wording is simplified: **Page content** is where we add the content, text, multimedia, or code

- **Options** gives us the choice of displaying the name and/or description of the page when a user clicks on it from our course.

- **Show** (as in Moodle 1.9) enables us during set up to specify if we wish this page to be visible yet or no. (It can quickly be changed later)

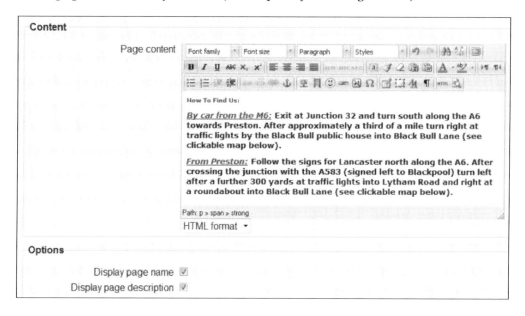

URL

The final link in the **Add a resource** menu is called **URL** and replaces the **link to a file or website** option. That option in earlier versions of Moodles has been split into two, with **File** as we saw earlier being the place to go to upload and display documents created elsewhere, and **URL** here being the selection to show websites we wish our users to access. This again simplifies creating course content for those not overly techie as it makes it more obvious which to choose — providing they know what URL means, of course.

Adding a link to a website with URL

When we click on **URL** from the **Add a resource** drop down, we get the editing screen, the top part of which is shown in the following screenshot:

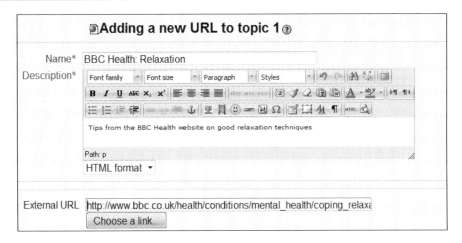

- The **Name** and **Description** fields are completed in the familiar way. We can decide further down whether to include them or not in the display.

- **External URL** is where we type in the website we wish our students to visit. If we don't know its name, we can open Google up in a new tab or window, locate it there and paste it in.

- Clicking **Choose a link...** would take us instead to the File Picker from where we could select a link from, say, YouTube or Flickr or any other repository our Moodle might have. (This is dealt with in *Chapter 3, Editing Text and Adding Files* and *Chapter 8, Admin Issues*)

- Scroll down to **Options** as shown in the next screenshot:

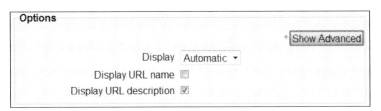

- **Display** allows us to choose how the URL will appear. We can choose from the following:

  1. **Automatic**: The site appears, replacing the window or tab of our Moodle

  2. **Embed**: The site appears embedded in a Moodle page with the navigation bar on top and, if we chose it, the URL description underneath

  3. **Open**: The site appears, replacing the window or tab of our Moodle

4. **In Pop-up**: The site appears in a new, popup window, keeping Moodle in the background. If this is selected, the **Show Advanced** settings page then permits us to define the size of the popup window.

5. **Display URL name** and **Display URL description** are options we can choose to include when the site is displayed with the **Embed** option

Summary

In this chapter, we've taken a tour of the drop-down menu **Add a resource** which appears when we edit our Moodle course pages.

We compared its earlier incarnation with the new Moodle 2.0 version and found that

- **File** now replaces **link to a file or website** and is the normal location to upload individual resources such as word-processed documents or slideshows

- **Folder** is the new name for the **display a directory** option

- **IMS Content package** is still available here with aesthetic changes

- **Label** now uses the enhanced TinyMCE HTML editor

- **Page** combines the previous **compose a text page** and **compose a webpage** options

- **URL** replaces **link to a file or website** and is the normal location to display weblinks we wish our students to access

Additionally, we've discovered that Moodle 2.0 gives us more control over who sees which resources and which filters are applied to them. For example, we could display an mp3 in one label with a player the student could click on to listen to and display it in another mp3 in a different label for them only to download.

If we edit any roles in any of our resources, we can see at a glance what our users are able to do by looking at the **Check permissions** option. We can thus avoid accidentally giving someone too many or too few permissions.

The **Restrict Availability** and **Activity Completion** settings, if enabled, can also help us control when students can access a resource based on date or having met certain criteria and allow us and them to track their progress through a course. For example, we can make it so they can only see a resource once they have achieved a certain percentage in an earlier activity such as a **Quiz.**

Moodle's **Quiz** is an example of an activity module that has been significantly upgraded in Moodle 2.0. In the next chapter, we will investigate what's new in the **Add an Activity** drop-down menu.

5
What's new in Add an Activity

In this chapter we will take a look at the **Add an activity** drop-down menu which appears on our course page when we have the editing turned on. We'll investigate how it has changed in Moodle 2.0 and concentrate on those features which have been improved.

Spot the difference...

The following screenshot shows, on the left, the Activity menu for Moodle 1.9 and, on the right, the latest version. There is not much to notice at first glance. The **Workshop** module, disabled in 1.9 is now enabled. What else?

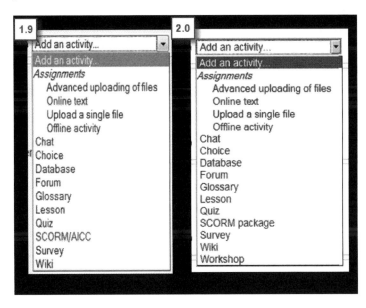

What's hiding?

- **Hot Potatoes**: Whereas before the **Hotpot** (Hot Potatoes) module was available but disabled by default (with its eye closed), in Moodle 2.0 it is now a contributed module and will need to be installed separately into your Moodle. It can be downloaded from `http://moodle.org/` | **Downloads** | **Modules and plugins**

- **Feedback**: A contributed module in 1.9 this is available in 2.0 but needs to be enabled (have its eye opened) in **Site administration** | **Plugins** | **Activity modules** | **Manage activities**. Eventually it will be replaced by a brand new module combining the best of both the **Feedback** and the **Questionnaire** modules.

What's changed?

While all the activity modules have been tweaked to ensure they are fully compliant with Moodle 2.0, three of them have been significantly enhanced. They are:

- **Quiz**: This has been made much more user-friendly.

- **Wiki**: Now Wiki 2 new design.

- **Workshop**: Hidden by default in our Moodle 1.9 as it needed a major overhaul. It's back better than ever before.

In this chapter, we'll focus on those three modules, starting with the Quiz. We shall also take a brief look at a useful feature in the **Assignment** module, a new **Forum** type, and the improved interface for **SCORM** activities.

Making a Moodle 2.0 quiz

Let's follow our teacher Andy as he creates a healthy Eating Quiz for our How To Be Happy course

Clicking on the **Quiz** link takes us to the new editing screen displaying the "front page" of the quiz:

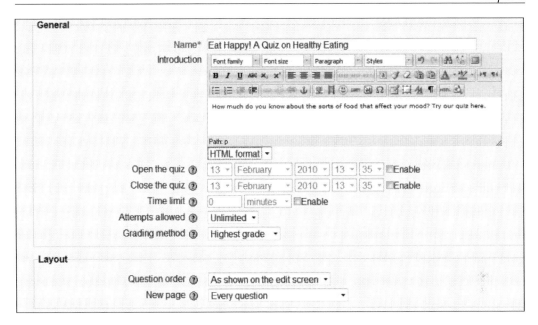

After a simplified naming and set up section we now have an improved **Layout** section, comprising the following:

- **Question order**: Here we can choose if we want the questions displayed as we created them or else appearing randomly

- **New page**: Here we can decide where we want the page breaks between questions to be

An extra feature in the **Display** section is the option to make visible the user's picture:

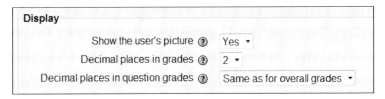

Why might we want that? Because selecting **Yes** as shown in the preceding screenshot will show the user's name and profile image on screen during the attempt and also on the review screen. If you are using the Quiz in exam conditions where you are invigilating, it makes it easier to check the user is logged in as themselves and hasn't paid an associate to take the test for them!

Note also that if **Restrict Availability** and **Activity Completion** have been enabled, then we'll be able to set those up here. You will find more on this in *Chapter 6, Managing the Learning Path*.

Where do we go from here?

Having decided upon the remaining settings for his quiz, familiar to us from Moodle 1.9, clicking on **Save and display** then takes Andy to the question making area where we'll follow him now:

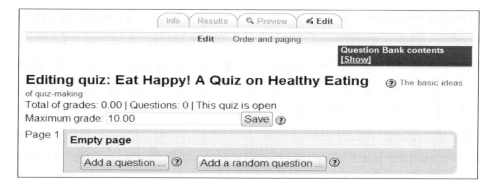

- **Question Bank contents**: This takes us to the categories and list of questions already made (if we have some) that we can choose from

- **Maximum grade**: The overall grade for the quiz is scaled to be out of this total

- **Add a question...**: This takes us to the question set up for making new questions

- **Add a random question...**: This allows us to set up the quiz so that when a student starts a new quiz attempt, a question is chosen at random from a particular category in the question bank

Creating questions for our quiz

Let's watch Andy make a couple of questions, one to a page, to get the idea:

Click Add a question

This brings up a list of question types to choose from:

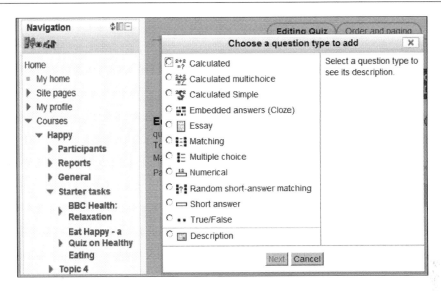

Select a question type and click **Next** at the bottom:

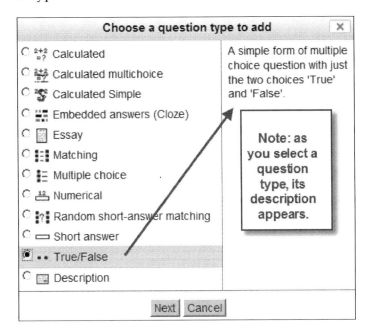

Add question details

The next screen allows us to ask the question, provide feedback to the user and wherever required correct and incorrect answers. This is not so different from creating questions in the earlier Quiz version, although we now have the advantage of the tinyMCE text editor we looked at in *Chapter 3, Editing Text and Adding Files*. What is new however, is the ability to "tag" a question:

Our course teacher, Andy, can add tags relating to this question and if the **Tags** block is added to the course, these key terms will appear.

 Andy's not the Moodle admin and so he can't add an **Official tag** which can be made available site wide, but if there is an official tag, it will appear in the top box.

Adding more questions

Once we've hit **Save changes** we're returned to the question set up area which now looks like this:

From here we can:

- **Edit the question**: By clicking the hand/pen icon as usual

- **Grade:** Use this to choose the mark for this particular question

- **Add question…**: This takes us back to the question set up page for making another question

- **Add a random question…**: This allows us to have a random question from questions previously made.

Ordering and displaying the quiz questions

Ok – Andy just added another question, a multiple choice type, and we now see the two questions with the icons giving us the option to move or delete on the right:

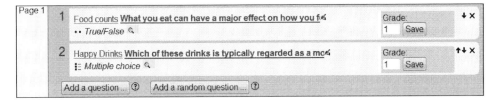

However, as seen on the left, both these questions are on Page 1. What if we wanted them on separate pages? We can organize the pages at any time during our quiz creation, either in the initial quiz set up screen or on the editing tab.

- **Move down:** We can use the down arrow to the right of question 2 to move it to the next page.

- **Quiz Layout**: Remember the **Layout** options when we first selected Quiz from the drop-down? Going back to it now with some questions created we can "repaginate" and tick/check the option we want, in this case, a new question per page:

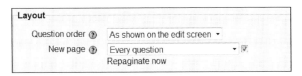

- **Order and paging:** Clicking those words from the **Edit** tab brings up the following screen:

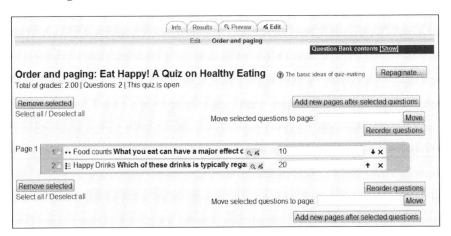

- **Repaginate**: This will let us choose how many questions per page we want in this case, 1 question per page.

- **Add new pages after selected questions**: If we select question 1 and hit this button, question 2 will appear on a page of its own.

What does the student see?

Our Healthy Eating quiz completed, let's log in as our student Emma to view it from her perspective. The first thing to notice as she enters the course is that those tags her teacher included appear in the tags block on the course page:

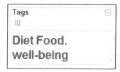

When Emma clicks on the Quiz link and starts her attempt, question 1 appears in a page of its own, as we'd planned. She also has a **Quiz navigation** block to the side showing her the number of questions she has:

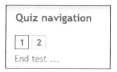

Emma also has an option to "flag" a particular question. The following screenshot shows where to flag it and then how the flag appears at the end of her quiz session:

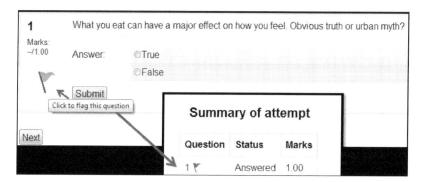

When she reviews her quiz, these questions are highlighted and her teacher will also be alerted to the fact that she felt certain items warranted flagging or bookmarking – for further study or discussion.

Making sure our students don't submit before they've answered all the questions

If Emma clicks **Next** at the end of the quiz, or if she clicks **End Test** in the quiz navigation block at any time, she's taken to a summary page where she can review her answers. Not only will this show which questions she's flagged but it will also enable her to check which (if any) questions she forgot to answer:

Eat Happy - a Quiz on Healthy Eating		
Summary of attempt		
Question	**Status**	**Marks**
1 ⚑	Answered	0.00
2	Answered	0.00

Once Emma completes the quiz she can review it. Not only can she review in the usual way, scrolling through the questions on the screen, but the boxes in the **Quiz navigation** also reflect her responses. A box will either be:

- **Flagged** – with a mark top right corner
- **Incorrect** – and colored pink
- **Correct** – and colored green

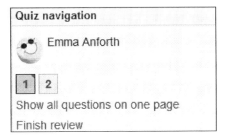

Question 1, which Emma flagged, she got wrong and it is colored pink. She got Question 2 right, so it is colored green. Imagine how useful this color-coded, flag-highlighting navigational feature would be if Emma had a quiz with a huge number of items!

The teacher's perspective

As in the earlier version of the **Quiz,** if he wishes to, Emma's teacher Andy can add a comment or override any grade Emma was allocated. Below is her incorrect response to question 1, and Andy just needs to click on the link to change her mark manually or respond to the fact she had flagged this question.

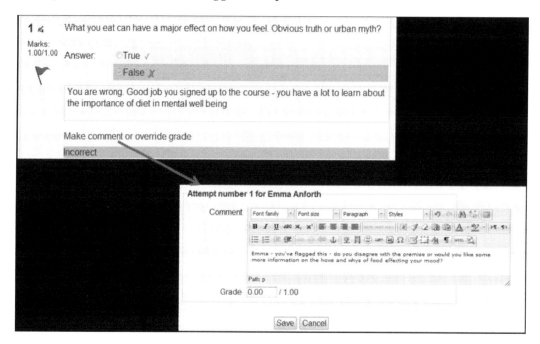

Making more quizzes

Of course, once a quiz has been taken by a student, it's no longer possible to add new questions to it. However, those questions we just made are now available for use in future quizzes should we want them. The question bank, as it's known, is easily accessible from the course administration block:

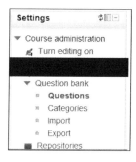

When creating a new quiz, we can click on **Question bank contents [Show]** to display previously made questions. The following screenshot reveals what we get when we click **[Show]**.

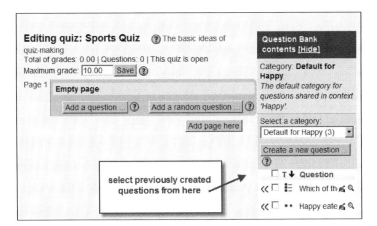

Sharing questions between courses

As a teacher in a course you can only add questions to categories you make for quizzes in that course. However, as an administrator you can also view and move questions from individual courses into their related course category and/or to the Moodle site as a whole.

Stuart Gorse, teacher of a Beginners' French course elsewhere on this Moodle, has a question that might fit well into our How To Be Happy course. As admin if I click on the **Questions** link in the Beginners' French course settings, I can move his question to the category or the system in order that Andy our teacher in the Happy course could use it:

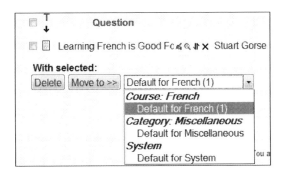

Quiz reports

Alongside improvements in the interface, the Moodle 2.0 Quiz has some changes to the quiz reports – very powerful features enabling advanced analysis of student responses. In brief:

- **Graphs** have been added to some reports to give us a quick overview of the results.

- The **Responses report** lets you download all students' answers to all questions. (This used to be an "optional extra" in Moodle –a non-standard, contributed report, but proved so popular it is now added to the main release.

- The new **Statistics report,** giving much more detailed information, has replaced the old Item Analysis report. More information on this is available here: http://docs.moodle.org/en/Development:Quiz_item_analysis_calculations

Recap on the Quiz

We've taken a look at the improvements to Moodle's Quiz. We've seen that:

- The set up page has been simplified
- Creating questions has been simplified
- It's possible to flag questions for later referral
- Questions can be accessed with one click in the post-quiz review and correct/incorrect questions are color-coded in an easy-to access navigation block

Making a Moodle 2.0 Wiki

Moodle's wiki has always been a very popular tool amongst students of all ages. In my own experience I have seen it used with primary school children as a means for collective story-telling and also in teenage students as an individual online exercise book. Teams of tutors have collaborated on wikis to share teaching ideas for their classes or design departmental schemes of work.

The new Wiki for Moodle 2.0 takes some elements from **NWiki**, a popular alternative to Moodle's default. Let's take a look at a wiki our teacher Andy made to encourage students to share experiences of different types of self-help methods. The initial setup looks like this:

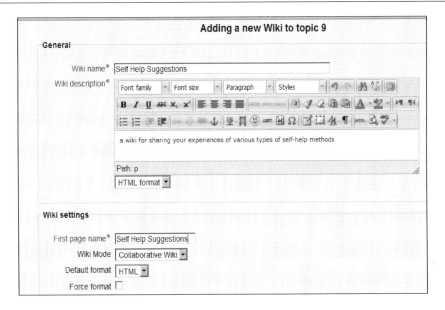

- **First page name***: This is offered us as our first page when the wiki is saved (see later)

- **Wiki Mode**: We can choose between **Collaborative Wiki** (as here where everyone may edit) or **Individual Wiki** (where each student edits their own)

- **Default format**: We can choose between the following markups:
    - **HTML the default and the one we'll use here**
    - **Creole**
    - **NWiki**

- **Force format**: We can check the box below to force our choice of format throughout the wiki.

Once the wiki is saved, we are taken to a screen asking us to create a page with the name we just chose:

When this first page is created, as below, it's interesting to note that:

- The tabs at the top are slightly altered from what we are used to (more on this later).
- We have full use of all the features in the new TinyMCE editor.
- We also have the ability to add tags.

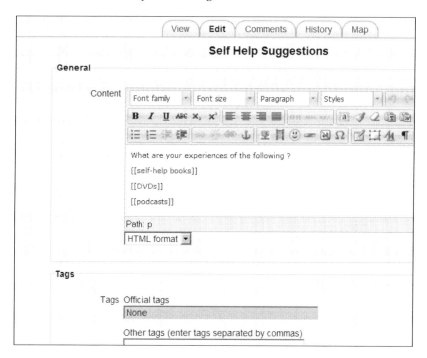

Adding new pages

With his current wiki settings, Andy creates new pages by adding double brackets around the words he wishes to have for his new page titles. When saved, these form links that can be clicked on to access a screen where a new page can be generated – just as with the initial page:

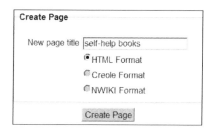

Our student Emma has made the first contribution to this page, as in the following screenshot:

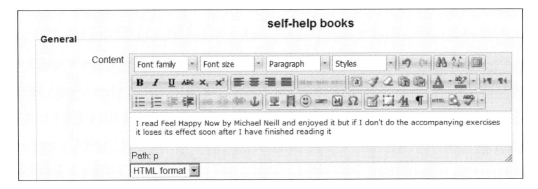

 Note that she could easily include sound, image, or video files in her entry by selecting the appropriate icon in the editor and accessing the file picker. She isn't limited either of course to items on her own computer but if the Moodle admin has enabled them – she can search a number of repositories such as Dropbox or Flickr.

What's new in the tabs

Leaving Emma's entry for a moment, let's take a brief tour of the tabs at the top of our wiki screen. In Moodle 1.9 the default set up gave us four tabs:

In Moodle 2.0, it's different:

View

This is the familiar tab where we can see the wiki.

Edit

This again is familiar to us as it's where groups or individuals can edit the contents of the wiki.

Comments

New to the wiki but not new to Moodle, we can – as in many other places! – comment on wikis. In fact, on Andy's course, feedback from comments is welcomed all over as the next screenshot shows (bottom right) his own course comments block in addition to the comments feature on the wiki.(We'll investigate **Comments** further in *Chapter 7, New Modules for Moodle 2*)

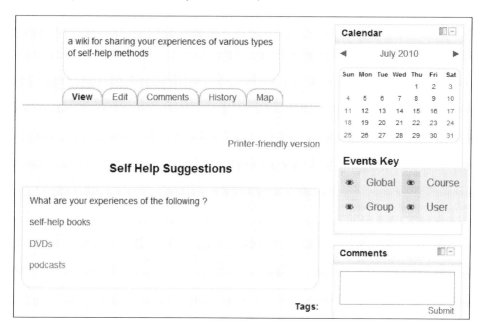

It is possible to comment on individual pages of the wiki. For instance, if we select the **self-help books** page that Emma just contributed to and then click the **Comments** tab there, we see that there are currently no comments:

This is soon remedied however, as manager Martin clicks **Add comment** and makes a remark:

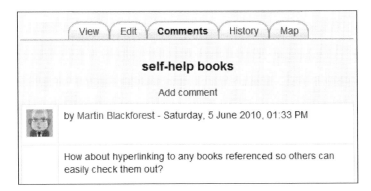

History

This is another tab we are familiar with from Moodle 1.9's wiki. We can see the history of the first page that Andy set up in the following screenshot:

Map

This is where we can navigate around our wiki:

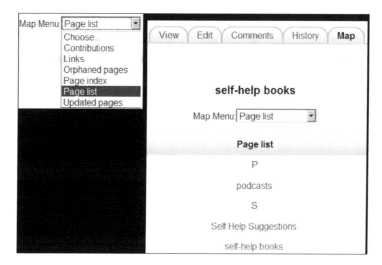

Recap on the wiki

The Moodle 2.0 wiki, still being developed, has:

- A more intuitive interface
- Choice of formats
- The ability to add comments
- More opportunities to display and embed media

What's new in the Workshop

Moodle's Workshop, a vehicle for peer assessment, has been radically overhauled for Moodle 2.0 In my experience it's a module people either use frequently and rate highly or stay well away from because of its complexity. Its reincarnation is both simpler to manipulate and also more powerful – so if you haven't used it before, now is a great time to try it out –and if you are a dedicated fan, you will be delighted with the improvements.

The best way to highlight the changes is to go off and see a workshop in action. Andy's making one where the students compose a poem which will then be assessed by the others in their class. As it is set up, if you have used Workshop before, you will notice a much neater, less confusing interface.

The set-up phase

From the drop-down menu, select **Workshop** and fill in the name and description details as shown in the following screenshot:

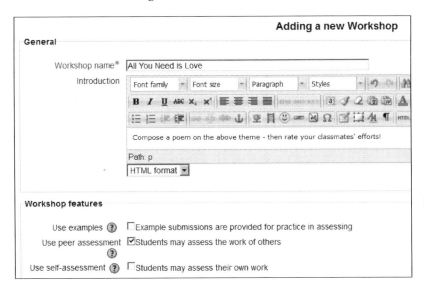

Workshop features

We can have three elements to our workshop:

1. **Use examples**: Students are provided with sample items that they can practice evaluating either before they send in their work or before they review others.

2. **Use peer assessment**: The "traditional" use of the workshop where students' work is distributed amongst them for them to evaluate.

3. **Use self-assessment**: Students reflect on and evaluate their own work.

Andy's only using the peer assessment feature in his, but it can be useful to have the others also.

Grading settings

Here's where Andy or we as teachers decide how this workshop will be graded:

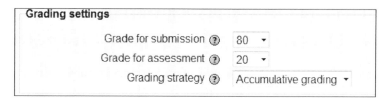

- **Grade for submission**: This is the mark the students will get for sending in their poem.

- **Grade for assessment**: This is their mark for evaluating others' work.

- **Grading strategy**: This is where we decide how the work will be graded and we can choose from:

  1. **Accumulative grading**: The default mark scheme where points are allocated for meeting certain criteria the teacher sets as assessment elements.

  2. **Comments**: Students add comments to the work rather than a numbered grade (this is the **no grading** of the older workshop).

  3. **Number of errors**: Students comment on and identify a number of errors in the work (this is the **error banding** of the older workshop).

  4. **Rubric**: Students fill in a rubric – a sheet with various marking criteria set out.

Submission and assessment settings

We then tell students how we want them to submit their work and how we want them to assess others. (If they are uploading items we can set here the number and size of any attachments) Andy just wants his students to type a poem directly into Moodle using the TinyMCE editor.

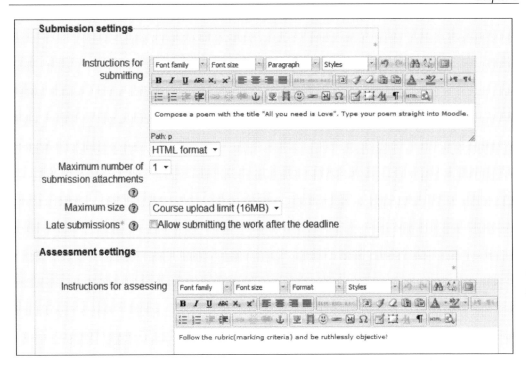

When and who?

- **Access control**: Which is hidden by default allows us to set the time of submitting and assessing.

- **Common module settings**: As usual – allows us to choose groups.

- **Restrict availability**: The setting to decide the conditions upon which students can access this workshop – we'll look at this in *Chapter 6, Managing the Learning Path*.

Clicking **Save and Display** takes us to the following screen:

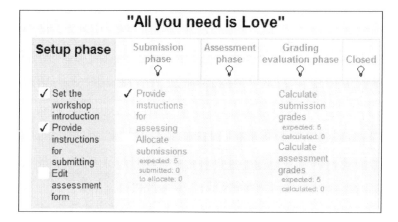

We're still in the set-up phase. Andy's done the first two tasks, so they are checked. He now needs to specify how he wants the students to review their classmates' work. Clicking on **Edit assessment form** takes us to the screen where that can be done, as shown in the following screenshot:

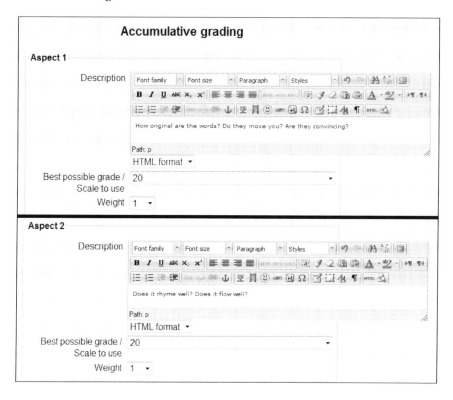

We set the criteria, choose the scale and weight. When our students do their peer assessment, they will get the finalized version of this form to complete.

 We selected **Accumulative grading**; had we chosen another grading strategy, its set up screen would also appear here.

The submission phase

Our screen now shows the set up phase is complete – time for Andy to turn on the "lightbulb" of the next phase ready for his students to submit their work:

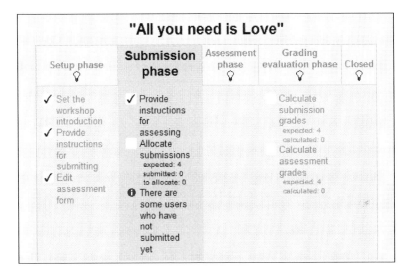

We've provided the instructions for assessing when we set the workshop up. The next stage is to allocate submissions – who will review what? This can be done now or we can wait till the students have sent in some work. Andy's going to wait....

How does the student submit their work?

Clicking on the workshop link as a student brings up the following screen. To submit their work they click the **Edit submission** link which should be familiar to us from the online text assignment:

Who assesses what?

Ok – the class has sent in their poems. We can see the uploads on our editing screen. Andy now needs to decide who gets whose poem to review:

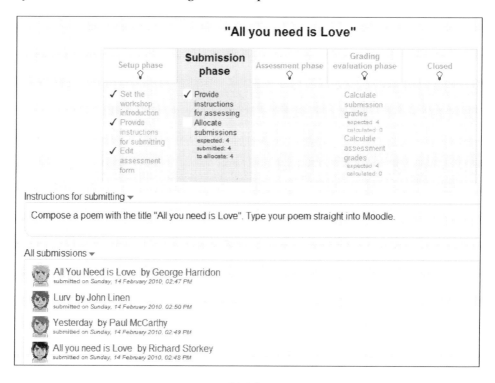

- Click **Allocate submissions**.
- Choose **Manual allocation** if you want to decide yourself who assesses whose work

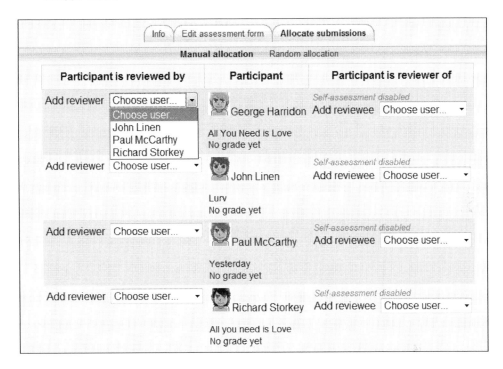

- Choose **Random allocation** if you want Moodle to do it for you.
- In **Allocation settings** decide how many items you want each reviewer to assess and whether they can assess even if they didn't submit any work:

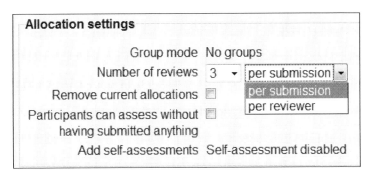

Moodle will then automatically assign reviewers to reviewees:

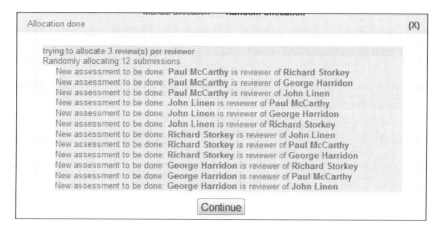

- In the set up screen we can now see at a glance who is reviewing whose work. We can manually alter Moodle's choices if we so wish.

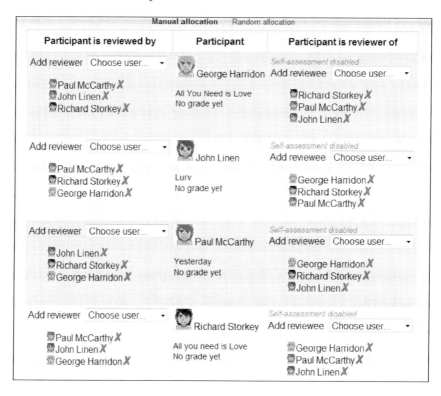

The assessment phase

With his users all allocated poems to assess Andy moves into the assessment phase and can turn on the light bulb to highlight – this column now changes to green.

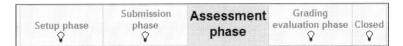

How do students assess each others' work?

Let's follow one of our students, George, as he re-enters the workshop to review his peers' poems. The following screenshot shows what he sees:

He has a link to the instructions for assessing and a list of students whose work he must review.

 Want to make it anonymous? You can prevent the group seeing each others' names by clicking on **Permissions** in the **Workshop administration** section of the **Settings** block. In **View author names** and **View reviewer names** click **X** next to **Student** to prevent these.

Clicking on **Assess** takes George to the assessment form we made for him to add his personal marks and comments:

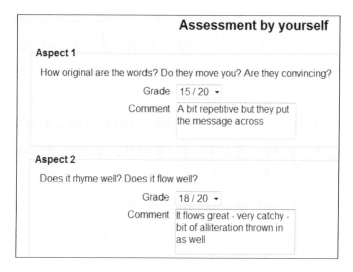

What the teacher sees

Andy, our teacher, can keep a close eye on how the assessing is going during this period as he gets a table with the students' names, what they submitted, which marks they have so far been allocated (and by whom) and which marks they have so far given to their peers.

Currently, only George has done any assessing and his grades are shown in the **Given grades** and **Received grades** columns.

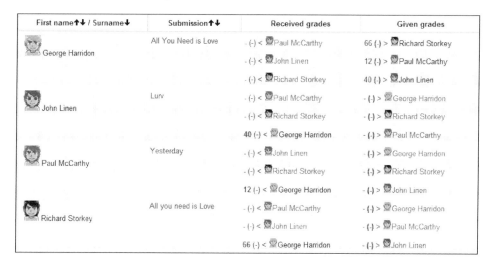

Weighting the assessments

In our example, the group is peer assessing without teacher input. It's perfectly fine as with the original Workshop for their teacher to assess too. It's also possible to add weightings to reviewers, so the teacher might wish to allocate more weight to his own assessment or to a particularly respected user within the group.

The grading evaluation phase

When the assessing time is over, we can start working out those marks! The next section turns green when Andy is ready to turn on the light bulb:

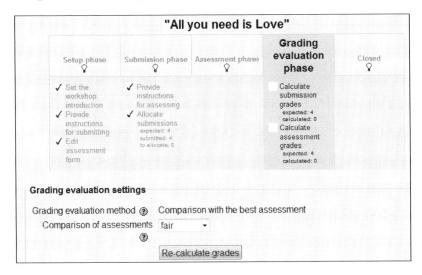

- **Grading evaluation method** and **Comparison of assessments** are currently (at the time of writing) the only options available and are the same as used in Moodle 1.

- **Re-calculate grades**: A teacher always has the final say on the marks given. Let's take a look at the grades now that Andy's group has completed their task.

First name↑↓ / Surname↓	Submission↑↓	Received grades	Grade for submission (of 80) ↑↓	Given grades	Grade for assessment (of 20) ↑↓
George Harridon	All You Need is Love	12 (9) < Paul McCarthy 72 (20) < John Linen 66 (20) < Richard Storkey	50	66 (20) > Richard Storkey 12 (17) > Paul McCarthy 40 (16) > John Linen	18
John Linen	Lurv	50 (20) < Paul McCarthy 40 (20) < Richard Storkey 40 (16) < George Harridon	43	72 (20) > George Harridon 44 (17) > Richard Storkey 24 (20) > Paul McCarthy	19
Paul McCarthy	Yesterday	24 (20) < John Linen 24 (20) < Richard Storkey 12 (17) < George Harridon	20	12 (9) > George Harridon 60 (20) > Richard Storkey 50 (20) > John Linen	16
Richard Storkey	All you need is Love	60 (20) < Paul McCarthy 44 (17) < John Linen 66 (20) < George Harridon	57	66 (20) > George Harridon 24 (20) > Paul McCarthy 40 (20) > John Linen	20

We have two extra columns now – the total grade for a student submitting their work, and the total grade for assessing others'. But what if we don't agree?

Teacher control

Seeing the overview of the grades given, our teacher Andy feels that maybe Paul was bit harsh on George contrasted with the other boys. Maybe they had an argument offline and Paul gave George a much lower mark for his poem. This is reflected also in Paul's lower assessment grade, which Moodle calculates according to how close a student is to the assessment grades of the others in the group.

Andy can go into Paul's assessment, override the grade, and offer an explanatory comment to Paul as to why he is lowering his assessment grade even further:

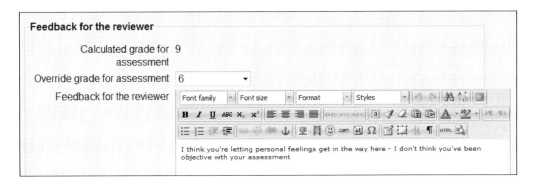

Re-calculate grades then alters the grades and shows the original and overridden mark:

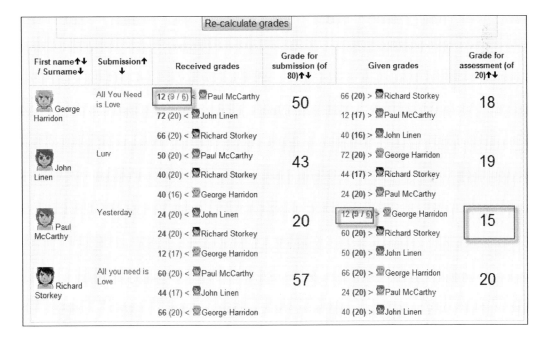

Our teacher Andy can also alter the final submission grade if he feels it is too low. If he clicks on George's submission he can then manually alter the grade (say to 70) and again, this alteration is reflected on the main screen. The original grades are red and crossed out; the new, overridden grades are green:

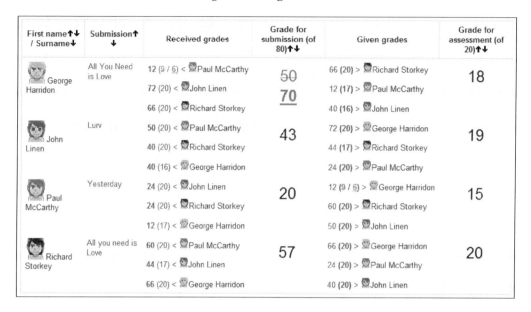

Additionally, there is a **Workshop Toolbox**:

This allows teachers such as Andy to:

- Reset the aggregated grades for submission and grades for assessment – and start all over again, basically.

- Reset the calculated grades for submission and grades for assessment. The information how the assessment forms are filled is still kept, but all the reviewers must open the assessment form again and re-save it to get the given grades calculated again.

A glance in the gradebook

Now the task is over, clicking on the **Closed** phase pushes the marks to Moodle's gradebook:

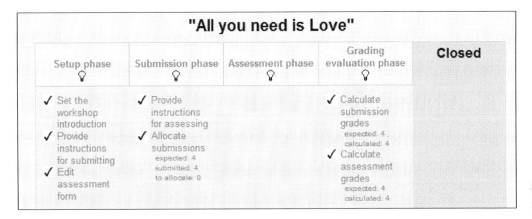

The Moodle 2.0 workshop differs from its earlier version in that it gives two grades – for submission and assessment. After that, it's up to you to tweak these results with whichever aggregation you prefer!

Where's the League table?

A popular feature of the older Workshop was the ability for Moodle to generate an automatic League table of the top assessed items in a class. That facility no longer exists as such but you can, as a teacher, manually choose who you want to display in your League table.

Recap on the workshop

We've taken a brief journey into the new style Workshop module for Moodle 2.0. We've seen that:

- It is clearly set out in different phases:
  - Set-up
  - Submission
  - Assessment
  - Grade evaluation
  - Closed

- There are opportunities not just for peer assessment but for individual self-evaluation too.

- The teacher has a total control over the path and grading of the workshop.

- Two grades – the submission and assessment grades – are recorded in the gradebook.

Other activity modules have benefited from enhancements too – let's take a look at three below:

Downloading assignments

The **Advanced Uploading of Files** and the **Upload a Single file** assignment types are very popular in many different sectors of the Moodle world. They allow students to upload documents in formats such MS Word or Open Office Writer which tutors may then mark and provide feedback on. One common complaint has been that if a tutor has a large class in UK schools it's not unheard of to have classes of 32+ for instance - and it's frustrating to have to download and grade each piece of work individually. Moodle 2.0 offers a solution to this, as we can see in an assignment set by Stuart on his Beginners' French course. When he clicks the **View... Submitted Assignments** link in order to mark them, note the link top right:

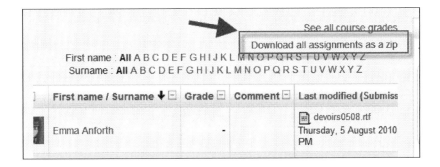

Clicking the link highlighted in the screenshot will prompt Stuart or any tutor to download a zipped folder of all the assignments in order to read and grade at leisure.

 This feature is also available for the **Online text** assignment – in which case, the assignments are saved as HTML (web) pages.

A new forum type

Moodle 2.0 offers a new way of displaying forum posts, alongside the four we're already familiar with:

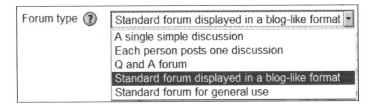

Standard forum displayed in a blog-like format

This forum is similar to the default **Standard forum for general use** in that you can start a new discussion topic, but the display is different and – as the title suggests – reminiscent of that of a blog. Let's remind ourselves first of the look of the Standard forum type:

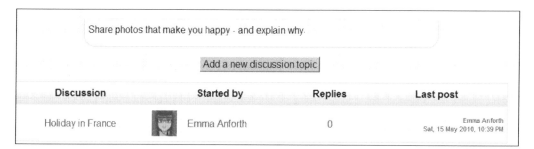

Notice that the discussion title is given, on the left, but with no actual content. After the poster's name comes a column giving the number of replies and the time of the last post. This is fine if we just want a quick glance at subject headings but what if we want actually to read the first post so we can decide if it's worth responding to? Here's a forum Andy started asking about **Inspiring People**. Other than selecting the new forum type from the drop-down menu, he set it up in the regular way, so we don't need to go into the details of it - but see how it looks on the page:

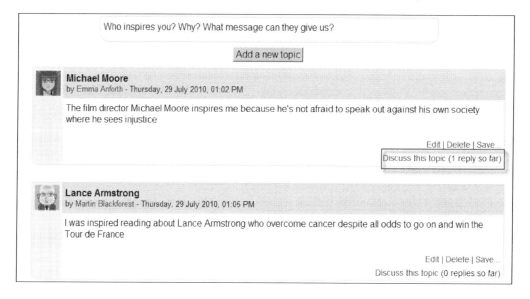

We get to read the starter topic in full and then, should we wish to comment on it, we click **Discuss this topic**. In the preceding example, one person has replied to Emma's post – here's what that screen looks like:

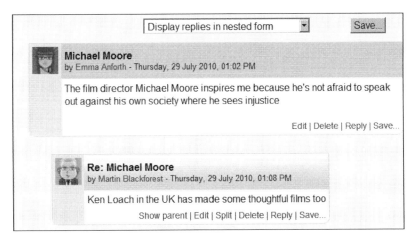

If we want to add our comments, we click **Reply** as normal.

 The **Save** option, as we discovered in *Chapter 3, Editing Text and Adding Files* is to enable a user to send their offering outside of Moodle to say, Google Docs or Mahara

Neater display of SCORM packages

SCORM (or **Shareable Content Object Reference Model**) is a popular method of delivering content to Virtual Learning Environments/Learning Management Systems such as Moodle. The advantage of a SCORM package is that it should transfer easily from one VLE/LMS to another. Commercial companies such as text book publishers have begun producing their materials as SCORM, enabling them to include more than just the written content. There are various free (eXe Learning) and bought for (Adobe *Captivate*) programs which allow tutors to create their own SCORM resources, should they wish. In Moodle 2.0, the SCORM player has had a major overhaul and now provides a much faster environment for users and fixes a range of display issues with the previous player. If we take a brief look at a SCORM activity in Andy's **How to Be Happy** course we can see this for ourselves.

- With the editing turned on, Andy chose **Add an activity | SCORM package**

- He clicked on **Choose a file...** to get to the file picker and upload his (zipped) SCORM package (in this case, a fun game from `http://www.contentgenerator.net/`).

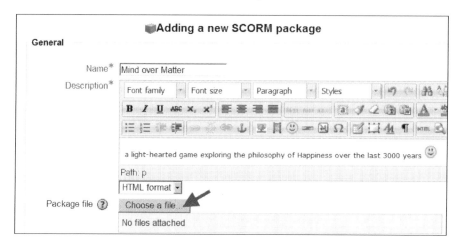

- He completed the other options as he would have in earlier versions of Moodle and clicked **Save and display**. If he had chosen to display the game on the same screen (rather than in a new window) then the resource shows as in the following screenshots:

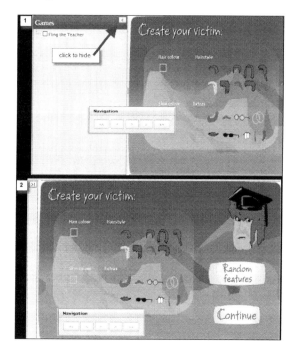

- Note the method of hiding the contents and also the new, "floating" navigation bar.

 Admin note: *There are other methods of selecting SCORM file types (such as* enabling an `imsmanifest.xml` URL to be specified) *in* **Site administration | Plugins | Activity modules | SCORM package**. *We'll check them out in Chapter 8, Admin Issues.*

Summary

In this chapter we've focused on the main improvements made in the **Add an activity** drop-down menu. These have been in the area of:

- Quiz
- Wiki
- Workshop

We also looked at a handy feature enabling us to download assignments in one go; a new way to display *Forum* posts and the improved *SCORM* interface.

During our exploration we came across the option: **Restrict Availability**. This is the brand new feature in Moodle 2.0 whereby we can set conditions upon which students can access items in our course. The following chapter deals with this feature, known as **Conditional Activities** and a related feature, **Completion Tracking**.

6

Managing the Learning Path

In this chapter, we'll look at how teachers can control their students' progress by making access to course activities dependent upon certain grades being obtained or certain conditions being met. This is a new feature called **Conditional Activities**. We'll also take a look at how students can see where they are up to in a course with the **completion (progress) tracking** setting and how a course can be marked as finished with the new **course completion** feature.

Why would we want to do this?

People learn in different ways: some read text books and follow the instructions step by step; some find videos (screencasts) helpful and some just like to dive in and play and learn from their mistakes. Increasingly, teachers try to assist their students' learning by offering them resources of various types in the hope that, with a combination of materials, one of them will hit the right button with an individual student.

I love Moodle because of the ease with which I can give my students text to read, podcasts to listen to, "how-to" movies to watch and interactive tasks to do. All these items are presented on the course page and students can go pick the one(s) they feel most comfortable with.

In my school we have classes organized according to the ability of the students. Yet on our Moodle courses, all students can see the work set for all the other classes. We use groups to make our gradebook neater but we don't use groupings to hide resources from certain classes. Where my course has activities of differing levels, I always leave them open so that, in theory, a student can go straight from a Level 1 exercise to a Level 3 exercise if they felt they needed stretching a bit.

Moodle was designed and developed according to the "Social Constructionist" philosophy. You can read more in the Moodle docs here http://docs.moodle.org/en/Philosophy

In short, Moodle is happiest when teachers are facilitating their students' learning, rather than lecturing to them. Moodle is happiest when students are in charge of their own learning, when they are discussing, collaborating, and actively "constructing" their own knowledge. They're finding their own path, rather than following a path set down for them by someone else.

However, some tutors – and their students - prefer a more structured, directed approach. One of the most popular feature requests for Moodle has been a method whereby a teacher can set their course so a student has to progress, step by step, from stage 1 to (say) stage 10, working systematically through stages 2 to 9 in between. Indeed, in commercial and public sector settings, tutors are often required to organize their courses in this manner. This is now possible in Moodle 2.0. So, if you want to give your students a rough guide and let them find their own way – you can! If you want to give them a detailed map with checkpoints they must reach along the way – you can!

Over the next few pages we're going to follow our teacher Stuart Gorse who's running a Beginners' French course. He feels he needs to set his exercises up in a highly directed way to avoid confusing his students. If they skip learning about the present tense and jump straight to the imperfect subjunctive – and then don't understand it – he feels they might get demotivated. He wants to control their learning path. So let's see how he sets it all up:

What admin needs to do

The features we're looking at in this chapter are not enabled by default, so whoever is admin on your Moodle needs to do the following:

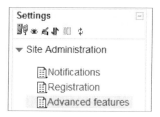

- Go to **Site Administration | Advanced Features** as shown in the preceding screenshot
- Enable **Completion tracking**
- Enable **Conditional Availability**
- Ensure **Progress tracking** is set for students

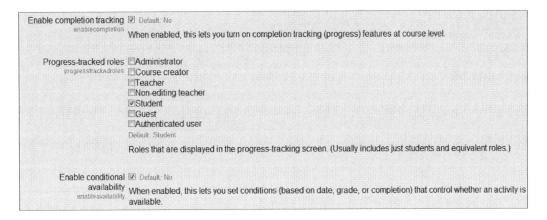

What the course teacher needs to do

Once the admin settings are enabled site wide, our teacher Stuart should then:

1. Go to the **Course Administration** block

2. Go into **settings**

3. Ensure student progress is shown by enabling **Completion tracking** in the drop-down menu as shown in the following screenshot:

4. Ensure **Completion tracking begins on enrolment** is checked (if he wants the course completion feature)

By doing this, Stuart is offering his class the chance to track their progress by having boxes to the right of each activity which will be checked as a student completes a task.

Setting up the tasks

Stuart, our teacher in the Beginners' French course, has decided he wants his students to access certain resources in a particular order as they get started. These are:

- An introduction to the course (in the form of a webpage). *Students have to read this before they can do anything else in the course.*

- A forum where students can introduce themselves. *They have to post a "hello" message before they can move on.*

- A quiz to gauge their prior knowledge. *They have to get 40% in a "how much do you know? quiz before they can tackle lesson 1.*

- The first French lesson. *They have to tackle this lesson before they can do the assignment.*

- The first French assignment based on lesson 1.

Viewed as a flow chart, we get this:

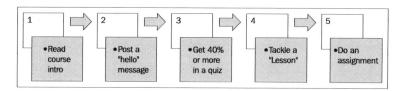

Once he has completed his work, the initial part of Stuart's course will look like the following screenshot:

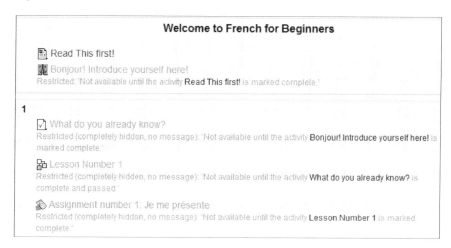

Note that the only activity currently visible is the **Read This first!** webpage. The others are grayed out, just as a hidden activity or topic section is normally in Moodle. If our students Andy or Emma look at the course, they see it like this:

They can see the introductory webpage but the forum is – tantalizingly - grayed out to them. They can see it's there but they can't yet access it. None of the other activities is visible at all. Andy and Emma will have to look at the **Read This first!** page first before they can join the forum – and they don't even know what else the course entails, because nothing is showing.

So how does Stuart achieve this? Let's go through step by step what he does:

Setting up the introductory webpage

Our teacher Stuart turns on the editing of his course. He then:

1. Selects the **Add a resource** drop-down

2. Chooses **page**

3. Adds the name and details he wants in the webpage (such as an introduction to the course)

4. Completes other information as he wishes

5. Scrolls down to the **Restrict availability** section.

For this first item, Stuart wants it to be available as soon as the students enroll in the course. So he doesn't set start or end dates and he sets to **(none)** the **Grade condition** and the **Activity completion condition**, as in the following screenshot:

Restricting when students see a resource: 1

Moodle 2.0 gives us a number of ways to restrict how students see a resource. We'll look at them below. First of all-let's not restrict it at all.

No restrictions

For this first item, Stuart wants it to be available as soon as the students enroll in the course. This is the default for each newly created activity - so he doesn't need to set start or end dates and he ensures the **Grade condition** and the **Activity completion condition** are set to **(none)**, as in the following screenshot:

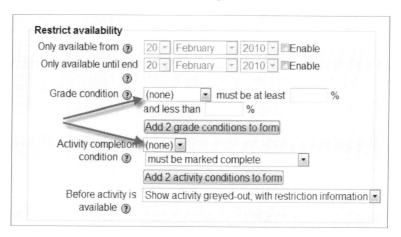

These settings ensure that **Read This first!** can be accessed at any time. It's not dependent on a date, an exam grade, or any other pre-requisite.

What does Only available from mean?

This is the setting to choose if you want particular dates when your activity can be accessed. Stuart doesn't want his dependent on dates but on other conditions – so he has left it at the default – which is always open. He'll set the conditions elsewhere.

What does Grade condition mean?

We'll see how Stuart sets a Grade condition a little later on. This is where we decide that a student is only able to move onto another task if they achieve a particular grade or come within a particular grade range in a previous activity.

What does Activity completion condition mean?

We'll see how Stuart deals with **Activity completion condition** in a moment. This is where we decide that a student is only able to move onto a certain task if they have fulfilled certain criteria in a previous activity. This might simply be viewing a page, reading a forum discussion, or actually posting in a forum.

The conditions for completion are context-sensitive, in other words, they change according to the type of activity presented.

What does Add 2 grade/activity conditions to form mean?

We're not tied to only having one grade a student must obtain or only one condition they must meet before they can move on. We can set several!

What does Before activity is available mean?

If a task has conditions upon it, we can decide whether to keep it totally hidden (so students have no idea it's there) or make it grayed out (so students can see it but can't access it until they've met the conditions.) In the Beginners' French course, Stuart has set the forum to **Show activity greyed-out, with restriction information**. This means Andy and Emma can see that there is a forum, but they can't post in it until they have first read his introductory page. Checking back at the screenshot showing us their view (image_05) it's obvious they don't know what's coming up after the forum. We'll see how Stuart sets the subsequent activities to be completely hidden shortly.

Restricting when students see a resource: 2

Lets now take a look at how we can set conditions:

Activity completion condition: Require view

Stuart wants to make sure his students read his introductory page before they post in the forum. He needs to do two things to make this happen:

- Set a **completion** condition on the **Read This first!** page

- Set an **availability** condition on the **Bonjour! Introduce yourself here!** forum.

- For the first condition, Stuart scrolls down his **Read This first!** settings, past the **Restrict Availability** section to the section called **Activity completion**:

What does Completion tracking mean?

This is where Stuart decides what will prompt Moodle to class the student's activity as "complete" so they can view their progress with the check marks at the side.

He chooses **Show activity as complete when conditions are met**. We'll see what the other choices are shortly and how they work. Now he needs to set the condition...

What does Require view mean?

This is the condition the students must meet in order to be able to access the forum. They must "view" the **Read This first!** webpage.

 Note that **Require view** simply means a user needs to click on the link to meet the condition. We still won't know whether Andy or Emma will actually read the introduction or not J

What does Expect completed mean?

This is merely a setting for Stuart to remind himself when students should have completed a task. It isn't seen by students and has no bearing on when or whether they complete the activity; it is just helpful to him to see if students are falling behind. The date is displayed only when viewing the progress report.

Ok – now to continue looking at how **Activity completion** can restrict when a student sees a resource, we need to follow Stuart into his second task- the forum:

Setting up the forum

Stuart set a **completion** condition on the **Read This first!** page. He now needs to set an **availability** condition on the *Bonjour!* forum. Here's how he does it.

With the editing turned on, he:

1. Selects the **Add an Activity** drop down
2. Chooses **forum**
3. Adds the type, name, and details he wants in the forum
4. Completes other information as he wishes
5. Scrolls down to the **Restrict availability** section

Let's take a look at the settings Stuart chooses and see if they make sense:

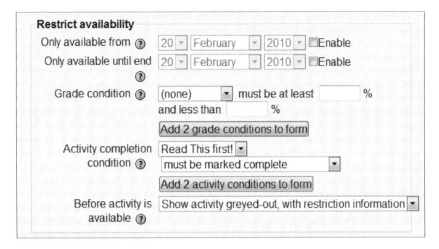

Grade condition

This is set to none because our students Andy and Emma didn't have to get a particular grade in the webpage they read; they just needed to read it (well – view it!).

Activity completion condition

This is set so that the webpage **Read This first!** must be marked complete. It will be marked complete when the students have viewed it – we know that, because Stuart our teacher entered that as the condition when he set up the page.

Before activity is available

This is set to show the forum *greyed-out but with restriction information*. In our case, the students can see that there is a forum but they are told they can't access it until they've read the webpage.

Ok – our forum and our webpage are now ready to go. Andy and Emma must read the page before they can see the forum:

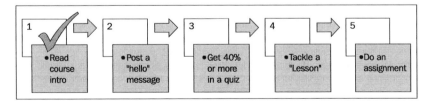

And then what? Where do we go from there? Looking at the preceding flowchart, let's have a recap on how Stuart wanted to control his students' learning.

- An introduction to the course (in the form of a webpage) *Students have to read this before they can do anything else in the course.*

- A forum where students can introduce themselves. *They have to post a "hello" message before they can move on.*

- A quiz to gauge their prior knowledge. *They have to take a "what do you already know?" quiz before they can tackle lesson 1.*

- The first French lesson. *They have to tackle this lesson before they can do the assignment.*

- The first French assignment based on lesson 1.

So the third item is a quiz to see how much French they already know. However, they can't do this quiz until they've introduced themselves on the forum. So again, Stuart needs to do two things to make this happen:

- Set a **completion** condition on the *Bonjour! Introduce yourself here!* forum

- Set an **availability** condition on the *What do you already know?* quiz

Restricting when students see a resource: 3

Let's take a look at another way of setting a condition:

Activity completion condition: Require post

We're still in the forum settings – if we scroll down below **Restrict availability** we come to the **Activity completion** section. Stuart's set it up like this:

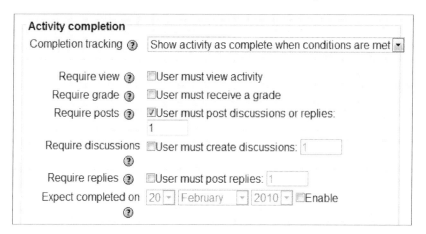

Completion tracking

This is where Stuart decides what will prompt Moodle to class the student's activity as **complete** so they can view their progress with the check marks at the side.

He chooses **Show activity as complete when conditions are met**. We'll see what the other choices are shortly and how they work. Now he needs to set the conditions...

Require view

As we saw with the **Read This first!** page, checking this means the students have to click on the link and take a look at the activity. However – because this time Stuart wants his students to actually post on the forum, he's going to leave this setting alone. Moodle will know that if Andy or Emma post in the forum then they are bound to have met the **Require view** condition, so that's OK.

Require grade

There's no grade in this forum, so Stuart leaves it unchecked.

Require posts

Stuart wants new students in the course to post at least once to introduce themselves to others – so he checks this.

Require discussions/require replies

Stuart isn't specifying whether his students must start new discussion or reply to others' – he just wants them to post – so he leaves this unchecked.

Expect completed

This is a handy date reminder for Stuart, as we saw in the **Read This first!** page settings.

Ok – now to continue looking at how **Activity completion** can restrict when a student sees a resource, we need to follow Stuart into his third task: the quiz.

Setting up the quiz

Stuart set a **completion** condition on the *Bonjour!* forum. He now needs to set an **availability** condition on the *What do you already know?* quiz. Here's how he does it.

With the editing turned on, he:

1. Selects the **Add an Activity** drop down
2. Chooses **quiz**

3. Completes other information as he wishes (he'll make the questions later)

4. Scrolls down to the **Restrict availability** section

Let's take a look at the settings Stuart chooses and see if our understanding' getting clearer:

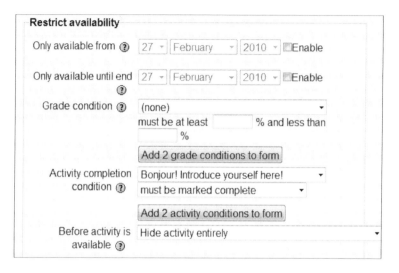

Only available from

This is where Stuart could set a date range for the quiz to be visible, but he leaves this as he sets conditions elsewhere.

Grade condition

This is where Stuart would specify a grade or grade range necessary before students could do the quiz –but this doesn't apply here.

Activity completion condition

This is where Stuart decides that students must have done *something* in the forum first before this quiz is visible to them. (We know what that *something* is because we saw that when he set the forum up he required them to post in it at least once.)

Once you have more than one activity in your course, you can choose from more than one item. If we look at that **Activity completion** condition drop down, we see that the first item-the introductory page – is also available:

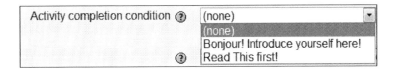

 However, we don't need to set the condition that Emma and Andy must view the introductory page – because that condition was already set for the forum – so it would be superfluous.

Before activity is available

This time, unlike before, Stuart has set it to **hide activity entirely**. This means the students won't know it even exists until they have posted in the forum. It will then magically appear! At the moment, this is what Stuart, our teacher sees:

Our flowchart shows where we've got up to in the plan:

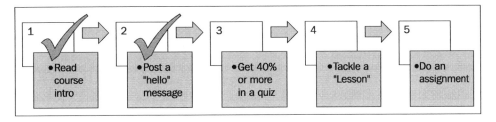

So far, we only required the students to view or contribute to a prior activity before allowing them to move on. However, with this quiz, Stuart actually wants them to obtain a specific grade in order to begin Lesson 1. Let's take a look at how he does that:

Restricting when students see a resource: 4

Here is yet another way to set a condition:

Activity completion condition: Require grade

Stuart wants his students to do a quiz to gauge how much French they already know. (This is going to help him later on in tailoring his materials to different ability levels). In order to even start the course by reading Lesson 1, they have to have obtained at least 40% in the quiz. So again, Stuart needs to do two things to make this happen:

- Set a **completion** condition in the *What do you already know?* quiz

- Set **availability** conditions in the *Lesson number 1* lesson

In addition, in order for the students' progress tracking correctly to display, he also needs to:

- Set a "pass" mark for the quiz in the gradebook.

We're still in the quiz settings – if we scroll down below **Restrict availability** we come to the **Activity completion** section: Stuart's set it up like this:

Completion tracking

This is where Stuart decides what will prompt Moodle to class the student's activity as "complete" so they can view their progress with the check marks at the side.

He chooses **Show activity as complete when conditions are met**. We'll see what the other choices are shortly and how they work. Now he needs to set the conditions...

Require view

As we saw earlier checking this means the students have to click on the link and take a look at the activity. However – because this time Stuart wants his students to actually do the quiz and obtain a grade, he's going to leave this setting alone. Moodle will know that if Andy or Emma do the quiz and get a grade, then they are bound to have met the **Require view** condition, so that's OK.

Require grade

Stuart wants his students to have done the quiz and obtained a certain grade before they get their progress check mark, so he selects this. *However – this alone won't do the job as we'll see in a moment!*

Expect completed

This is a handy date reminder for Stuart, to keep an eye on his students' progress, as we saw in the earlier settings.

Setting a pass or fail grade condition

If we leave the activity completion settings as they are now, our students will get a check to tell them they've completed the quiz whether they get 5% or 95% simply because they have met the condition **Require grade**. However, Stuart intends to set the availability conditions in Lesson 1 such that they won't be able to access the quiz unless they get 40% or more. This will confuse Andy and Emma. If the quiz is marked as completed, why can't they start the lesson?

We need to tinker a bit with the gradebook first to sort this confusion out. We need to make it so that the quiz is only shown as completed if the students get 40% or more. To do that, we need to set the pass grade for this quiz to 40% in the gradebook. Here's how Stuart does it. He heads for **Course Administration** as shown in the following screenshot:

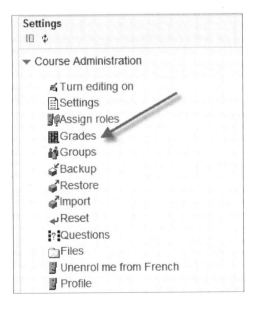

After this he needs to:

1. Click on **Grades**
2. Select **Edit categories and items**
3. Click the edit (pen/hand) icon next to the activity (for Stuart, the quiz as in the screenshot below)

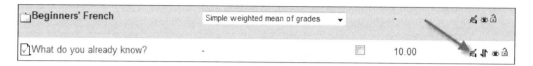

4. Click **show advanced** on the screen that comes up next
5. Set the **Grade to pass** to the desired grade (for Stuart, 4.0)

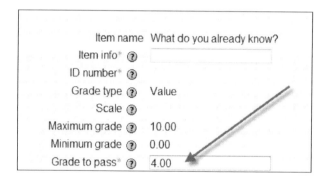

6. Save the changes.

Ok – now to continue looking at how **Activity completion condition** can restrict when a student sees a resource, we need to follow Stuart into his fourth task: Lesson number 1.

Setting up the Lesson

Previously in Moodle, the **Lesson** module was the only place we could easily set conditions. In Moodle 1.9 I'd often use a **Lesson** if I wanted to control my students' learning path. I won't need to do this so often now, as **Conditional Activities** will do the job for me in other modules too.

Stuart set a **completion** condition on the *What do you already know?* quiz. He went into the gradebook and set a pass mark for the quiz. Now his students will only get the quiz showing as completed if they obtain 40% or more.

He now needs to set **availability** conditions on *Lesson number 1*. Here's how he does it.

With the editing turned on he:

1. Selects the **Add an Activity** drop down

2. Chooses **Lesson**

3. Completes other information as he wishes

4. Scrolls down to **Restrict availability**

5. Let's take a look at the settings Stuart chooses. Hopefully by now the penny should be starting to drop!

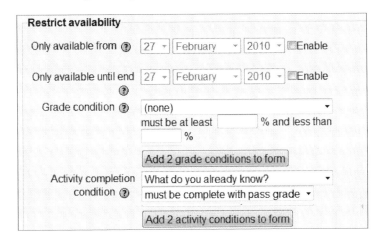

Let's just focus this time on the two main elements:

Grade condition

Stuart could use this setting to determine when his students can view the lesson. He could set the **grade condition** to must be at least 40%, (we'll look shortly at when he might want to use this feature) but instead he's using the below:

Activity completion condition

This is where Stuart sets it so that the students must have passed the quiz (that is, got 40% or more) in order for the quiz to be checked as *completed*.

Note: the other Activity completion conditions are:

Must be marked complete

Must not   be marked complete

Must be complete with pass grade

Must be complete with fail grade

If we go to the course page and look at the course now, from Stuart's point of view, this is what we see:

As we've already seen, the students will only see the introductory page and the grayed out forum.

Where do we go from there? Let's refer back to our flowchart and just recap how Stuart wanted to control his students' learning.

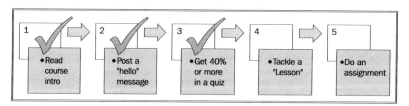

He wanted:

- An introduction to the course (in the form of a webpage) *Students have to read this before they can do anything else in the course.*

- A forum where students can introduce themselves. *They have to post a "hello" message before they can move on.*

- A quiz to gauge their prior knowledge. *They have to take a "what do you already know? quiz before they can tackle lesson 1.*

- The first French lesson. *They have to tackle this lesson before they can do the assignment.*
- The first French assignment based on lesson 1.

We've got as far as item 3 – the first French lesson. Before they can do the first French assignment they have to tackle the lesson. Hopefully by now you will be able to work out what Stuart did to his lesson and assignment to make this happen, so we won't dwell on them in great detail:

He needed to do two things:

- Set a **completion** condition in the Lesson number 1 lesson
- Set an **availability** condition in the Assignment number 1 assignment

In the lesson, he set the **Activity completion condition** to **Require view**.

In the assignment, he set the **Restrict availability condition** to Lesson number 1 *must be marked complete.*

How can students track their progress?

As we've followed Stuart round studying how he sets up his course tasks, we've noticed in the **Activity completion** section a drop-down called **Completion tracking.** If this setting is turned on by admin, it's where the teacher decides what will prompt Moodle to class the student's activity as "complete" so they can view their progress with check marks at the side. Let's take a look now at this dropdown and the effect it has on a student's course page.

The completion tracking options

This menu has three options, as we can see in the next screenshot:

- **Do not indicate activity completion**: This will not display a check and students will not be able to gauge their progress.

- **Users can manually mark the activity as completed**: This puts the onus on the student to keep track of their progress by checking when they feel they are done with an activity.

- **Show activity as complete when conditions are met**: This is where Moodle automatically shows the task as completed once students have fulfilled various criteria. This is the one Stuart has used so far in his course.

What does a student see?

When Andy, Emma or any student logs into the course they see a help button on the top right corner. Clicking on it explains to them how the completion (progress) tracking system works:

If it's been switched on by admin, then students will get either a dotted check or a blank box next to each activity.

- A **dotted check mark** is one they can manually click on to mark an activity complete when they feel it's done

- A **blank box** will automatically show a check when Moodle decides the activity is completed. If a student moves the cursor over the blank box it will show **not completed**.

Automatic tracking

If we take a look at student Andy's view when he starts the course, we can see this in action next to the **Read This first!** page. In the next screenshot, I've drawn a square around the blank box as it's difficult to see on some themes. With the cursor hovered over it, it tells me this activity hasn't yet been classed as complete:

If Andy goes and reads (views) the page, the box will then automatically show a check. You'll recall we watched how Stuart set this up earlier on in this chapter. He set the activity completion condition and completion tracking on the page thus:

Once Andy has looked at that introductory page, the appearance of his course changes. He has a check next to the page, showing him he's completed that task and the forum is no longer grayed out – it's visible and available for him to post in!

Again, I've drawn squares around the check boxes as they are not easy to see on the screenshot.

When Andy has posted in the forum – this is what he sees when he goes back to the page:

A check has appeared next to the forum – and the **What do you already know?** quiz is now visible for him to attempt.

Of course – he will only get a check in the third box if he obtains 40% more on the quiz. And he will only be able to access the first lesson if he obtains 40% or more on the quiz.

Manual tracking

Well, Andy did obtain over 40% in the quiz and was then able to see Lesson number Once he'd completed that first lesson, his first assignment was revealed to him. Here's our flow chart again:

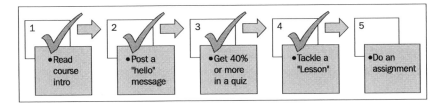

If we take a look at the page now, we can see a slightly different checkbox next to the assignment:

This is the dotted check which Andy can manually mark as complete if he thinks he's done what's required of him. Unlike the automatic tracking, with the blank box, if he moves his cursor over the check, he gets a prompt to mark as complete:

When this checkbox is marked as complete, the box looks slightly different from the other – automatic –ones, as we can see in the next screenshot. This is to make it easier to tell the difference between what has been automatically tracked and what Andy has manually checked off:

 In my theme, the automatic checkbox is on a white background; the manual checkbox is on a grey background. However the background colors are theme dependent.

Differentiating with conditional activities

We've seen how Stuart can control the learning path of the students on the Beginners' French course by making use of the new feature in Moodle known as **Conditional Activities**. We've also seen how students can track their progress with checkmarks at the side of each task.

With some imaginative use of **Conditional Activities**, teachers could allow students to select and branch out into different learning paths according to preferences or grade results. Once the student has set off, they don't then see the alternative paths and other tasks their classmates might be attempting. This can already be done in Moodle by using the grouping facility. Using **Conditional Activities** is just another means to the same end. You can find more suggestions for this in the Moodle docs `http://docs.moodle.org/en/Conditional_activities#Tricks_and_techniques`

Here are two suggestions for using **Conditional Activities** to differentiate, the first in Stuart's *Beginners' French* course and the second in Andy's *How To Be Happy* course.

Differentiating with a grade condition

As it is now, if any student in the Beginners' French course gets 40% or more they can access Lesson 1. However – what if Stuart wants to split those with greater prior knowledge from those with less prior knowledge? He could have a *Basic Lesson1*, for those who scored fewer marks in the *"how much do you already know?"* quiz and an *Intermediate Lesson 1* for those who scored slightly better. The flowchart below shows the path:

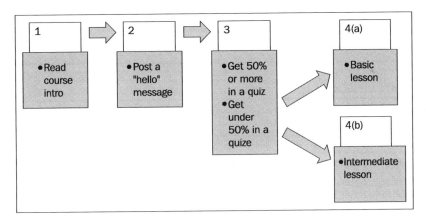

Stuart needs to do two things to make this happen:

- In the quiz, set the **Activity Completion** condition as **Require grade** but without a pass/fail. Students will see the "completed" check as long as they attempt the quiz

- Set **Restrict Availability** conditions in a **Basic Lesson** and an **Intermediate lesson** as follows:

Basic Lesson grade conditions

If students score less than 50% in the quiz, Stuart wants them to be directed to the Basic Lesson:

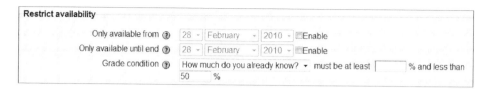

Intermediate Lesson grade conditions

If students score 50% or more in the quiz, Stuart wants them to be directed to the intermediate lesson:

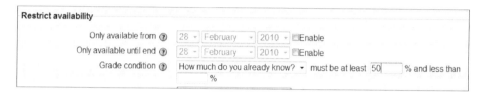

If we now look at the course page from the teacher's point of view, this is how it looks:

We don't need to check the student's view because we already know both lessons will be invisible until they obtain a certain score in the quiz! However – Stuart can now easily tailor the rest of his course to a *Basic* or an *Intermediate* student by relating the **Restrict availability** conditions of subsequent lessons and assignments to either the *Basic* or the Intermediate lessons.

Differentiating with a forum post

We've already seen how we can set a condition that a student has to post in a forum before they can access the next task or activity. In Stuart's French course, Andy and Emma had to introduce themselves before they could tackle the quiz.

We can use this technique to organize a grouping system for students who wish to choose a particular project to undertake or module to study. Andy has done this in his *How to Be Happy* course. He wants students to choose whether they would like to learn about how keeping fit and eating healthily can make you happy – or whether they'd prefer to study how meditation can bring inner peace. He has set up two forums. Students must choose one and post in there to let Andy know which module they are opting for.

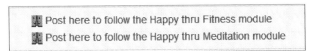

So far, so good. So what happens when Emma posts on the *Happy through Meditation* forum? She gets the following view:

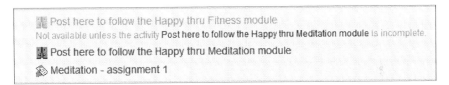

Her first assignment on mediation is now visible. We can understand that, because Andy will have set up the conditions on the assignment such that, if Emma posted in the Meditation forum, she'd be allowed access to the Meditation assignment.

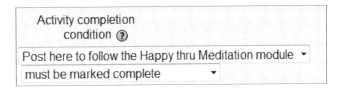

But what's happened to the other forum, the Fitness forum Emma didn't choose? It is now grayed out, with the condition *Not available unless the activity* **Post here to follow the Happy thru Meditation module** *is incomplete.*

In other words, a student can only choose one module by posting in the relevant forum – once they've posted – the other forum becomes locked to them with a **Restrict availability** condition. Clever, yes? The three steps in the following flowchart illustrate this:

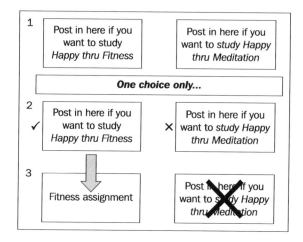

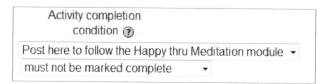

Andy went into the Fitness forum and set the availability thus:

He then went into the Meditation forum and set the availability thus:

So a student can only post in the Fitness forum if they haven't posted in the Meditation forum already. And they can only post in the Meditation forum if they haven't already posted in the Fitness forum. Once they post in one, the other is no longer available.

Let's just double check that with a different student who, unlike Emma, is interested in the **Happy thru Fitness module**. He posts in the Fitness forum to let Andy know this is the group he wants to be in:

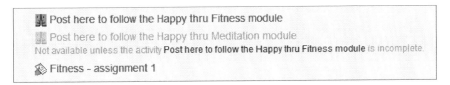

He gets the opposite of Emma – as he should and as Andy wanted. Now he can set off on his private journey to happiness via fitness while Emma sets off on her meditational path – and, on Andy's course page at least, never the twain shall meet!

Marking a course as "Complete"

Finally, let's look at how a course can be officially classed as finished - if our learning can ever be considered to be "finished" that is! For this to happen, a teacher needs to have enabled **Completion tracking** and checked/ticked the **Completion tracking begins on enrolment** box in the course settings as we saw at the start of the chapter:

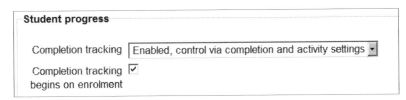

This will add a new link to the course settings: **Completion tracking**.

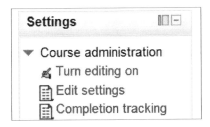

Let's click on the link and take the items a few at a time:

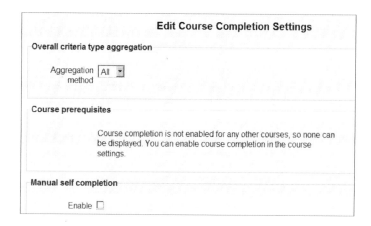

Overall criteria type aggregation

We can choose from **All** (that is, all tasks must be completed) or **Any** (that is, a selection).

Course prerequisites

Here we can set our current course so that students need to have completed a previous course first. In this instance, no other courses have got course completion enabled so this isn't possible, but later on we'll see what happens if it is enabled.

Manual self completion

Courses may be declared complete either manually by the student themselves or by the teacher or following certain specified criteria. In this setting, we can allow our students to mark the course as finished themselves by checking this box.

Manual completion by

Instead of the student marking the course as finished by himself/herself, we can have another user such as a Teacher or Manager doing so.

Activities completed

Below here is a list of all the tasks on our course. We select the ones we want included in our criteria for completion and, as mentioned before, decide if we want the Aggregation method to be for **All** or **Any** of these.

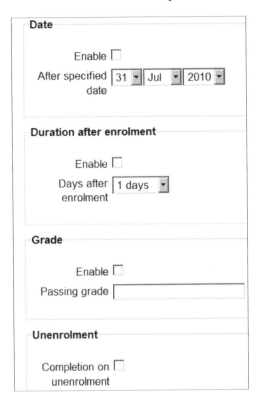

Date

We can specify Course Completion according to a calendar date here.

Duration after enrolment

We can set a course to be complete after a certain period of time following students' enrolment here.

Grade

This is where we can make Course Completion dependent on a particular final "passing" grade having been obtained.

Unenrolment

Here is where we can declare that Completion takes place once a student is no longer enrolled in the course.

Course Completion in Practice: Example 1

Our teacher of the How to Be Happy course, Andy, has set the course so that students can manually mark it as complete. How did he do it?

He checked the **Enable** Manual self completion box we saw earlier:

1. He added a block **Self Completion**, as shown in the following screenshot. This gives Emma and other students a link where they can register their course as complete.

2. He added a block **Course Completion status** as shown in the following screenshot. This gives Andy a quick overview of where students are up to on the course and gives each student an individual view:

Now let's view these blocks from our student Emma's point of view and see how she can check the course off as "done".

What does a student see? How can they self-complete?

Emma is enrolled in the **How to Be Happy** course and teacher Andy has set it so that students can mark the course as complete themselves. When Emma logs in she sees the two blocks thus:

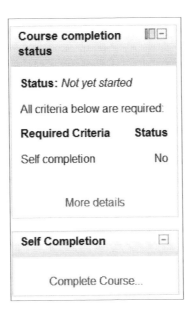

In order to meet the required criteria in the **Course completion status** block, Emma needs to click the link **Complete Course…** in the **Self Completion** block. On clicking it, she gets the following confirmation request:

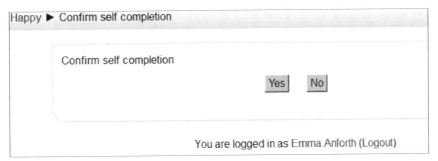

The course will be confirmed as complete at the next cron job and Emma sees the following notification:

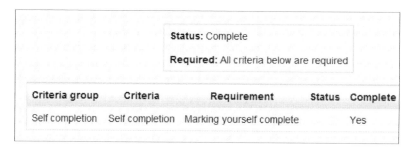

If teacher Andy accesses the report now in the **Course completion status** block he sees student Emma's status as below (that is; she's completed the course):

Criteria group	Self	Course
Aggregation method	-	All
Criteria	Self completion	Course Complete
First name / Surname		Course
Emma Anforth	✓	✓

In the preceding example, a student was able manually to mark a course as complete. What if a teacher wants the course only to be officially complete once a student has finished a certain number of activities or obtained a specific grade? What if a teacher wants to ensure a student has undertaken a course elsewhere on the site before moving onto theirs? We'll go now to our Beginners' French course where Stuart wants to do just that:

Course Completion in Practice: Example 2

Because Andy set completion tracking on his course, that course becomes available as a prerequisite for Stuart when he clicks on the **Completion tracking** link.

1. Stuart chose this as a prerequisite for his course. Students like Emma won't be able to have their French course marked "complete" until they have shown that they have finished Andy's course:

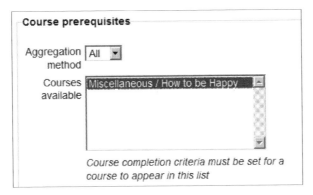

2. Additionally, Stuart doesn't want his students to use the self-completion option for his course. Instead, he wants them to have tackled three assignments, so he checked these in the **Activities completed** section:

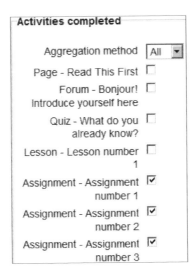

What does a teacher see?

When Stuart looks at the **Course completion status** block at the start of the course, this is what he sees:

Criteria group	Prerequisites	Activities			Course
Aggregation method	All	All			All
Criteria	How to be Happy)	Assignment number 1	Assignment number 2	Assignment number 3	Course Complete
First name / Surname	Happy	Assignment	Assignment	Assignment	Course
Emma Anforth	✓	✓	✓	✓	✓
Andy Field					

Emma finished the How to Be Happy course by marking it complete herself – so that prerequisite is checked. Once she has done the other necessary tasks they will be checked too and Stuart's view will change accordingly:

Criteria group	Prerequisites	Activities			Course
Aggregation method	All	All			All
Criteria	How to be Happy)	Assignment number 1	Assignment number 2	Assignment number 3	Course Complete
First name / Surname	Happy	Assignment	Assignment	Assignment	Course
Emma Anforth	✓	✓	✓	✓	✓
Andy Field					

What does a student see?

When student Emma looks at the **Course completion status** block at the start of the course, this is what she sees:

Criteria group	Criteria	Requirement	Status	Complete
Activities completed	Assignment number 1			No
(*all* required)	Assignment number 2			No
	Assignment number 3			No
Prerequisites completed	How to be Happy	Course Completed	See details	Yes

When she has met the other criteria in Stuart's course (and after the cron job) the block will show her status as **Complete**:

If she clicks on the **More details** link at the bottom, she will see her achievements thus:

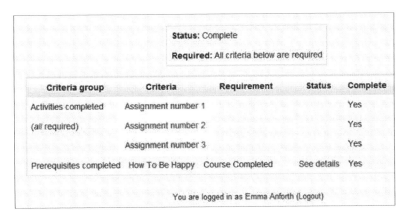

Summary

In this chapter we've looked at two new features of Moodle 2.0 that help teacher and students manage their learning:

- **Conditional activities**: A way to organize a course so that tasks are only available dependent on certain grades being obtained or criteria being met beforehand.

- **Completion tracking**: A way for students to have checkboxes next to their tasks that are either automatically marked as complete or which students themselves can manually mark if they feel they've finished the exercise – or alternatively a way for whole courses to be checked off as finished.

We looked at a couple of ways **Conditional Activities** can be tweaked to allow a teacher to differentiate the learning path in a course, according to a grade a student gets or a selection they make.

Conditional Activities is a very powerful feature and will no doubt prove very popular. However, it is worth thinking twice before you rush in. I quote from the Moodle docs below:

Discussion: Should you really use conditional activities?

Conditional activities are a way for you to force your students to do things in a certain order. Is that really what you want? The answer will depend on your particular circumstances, but it is worth taking a moment to reflect upon the degree to which conditional activities are appropriate for your course.

Cautions

It is certainly good course design to make it clear to your students what they are expected to do next, to give good guidance. But do you need to use force? Might it not be better to leave students in control of their own learning and just use labels and layout, rather than locks and keys to suggest the best path?

Finally, we explored the **Course Completion** feature whereby a course can be marked as "complete" either manually or based on certain pre-designated conditions and looked at two examples of this.

The main focus of this chapter has been on directing the students' learning and progress through a course. Our next chapter puts the power back into the students' hands by investigating the different ways in which they can *Have Their Say* in Moodle 2.0.

7
Having your say

In this chapter, we'll look at how communicating and expressing yourself has been made easier in Moodle 2.0. The "social networking" aspect of Moodle was somewhat limited in the earlier versions, but is now much enhanced. In addition to the inclusion of the popular Feedback module, we'll look at changes in messaging and a new **Comments** feature which enables you to comment on Moodle blogs—and comment pretty much anywhere else too!

Blogs—before and after

There has always been a blogging option in a standard Moodle install. However, some users have found it unsatisfactory because of the following reasons:

- The blog is attached to the user profile so you can only have one blog
- There is no way to attach a blog or blog entry to a particular course
- There is no way for other people to comment on your blog

For this reason, alternative blog systems (such as the contributed OU blog module) have become popular as they give users a wider range of options.

The standard blog in Moodle 2.0 has changed, and now:

- A blog entry can optionally be associated with a course
- It is possible to comment on a blog entry
- Blog entries from outside of Moodle can be copied in
- It is now possible to search blog entries

Let's go to our Moodle 2.0 site and see how our student, Emma, handles blogging.

Where's my blog?

Last year when Emma studied on Moodle 1.9, if she wanted to make a blog entry she would click on her name to access her profile and she'd see a blog tab like the one shown in following screenshot:

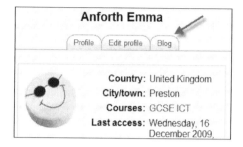

Alternatively, if her tutor had added the blog menu block, she could click on **Add a new entry** and create her blog post there as follows:

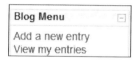

The annoyance was that if she added a new entry in the blog menu of her ICT course, her classmates in her Art course could see that entry (even, confusingly, if the blog menu had a link to entries for just that course).

If we follow Emma into the Beginners' French course in Moodle 2.0, we see that she can access her profile from the navigation block by clicking on **My profile** and then selecting **View Profile**.

(She can also view her profile by clicking on her username as she could in Moodle 1.9). If she then clicks on **Blogs** she can view all the entries she made anywhere in Moodle and can also add a new entry:

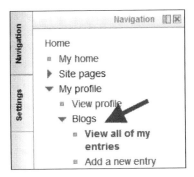

As before, Emma can also add her entry through the blog menu, so let's take a look at that. Her tutor, Stuart needs to have added this block to the course.

The Blog Menu block

To add this to a course a teacher such as Stuart needs to turn on the editing and select **Blog menu** from the list of available blocks:

The **Blog menu** displays the following links:

- **View all entries for this course**: Here's where Emma and others can read blog entries specific to that course. This link shows users all the blog posts for the course they are currently in.

- **View my entries about this course**: Here's where Emma can check the entries she has already made associated with this course. This link shows users their own blog posts for the course they are currently in.

- **Add an entry about this course**: Here's where Emma can add a blog entry related only to this course. When she does that, she is taken to the editing screen for adding a new blog entry, which she starts as shown in the following screenshot:

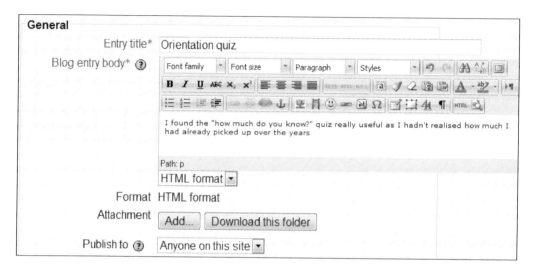

Just as in Moodle 1.9, she can attach documents, choose to publish publicly or keep to herself and add tags. The changes come as we scroll down. At the bottom of the screen is a section which associates her entry with the course she is presently in:

Once she has saved it, she sees her post appear as follows:

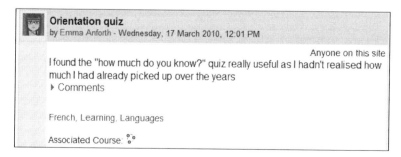

- **View all of my entries**: Here Emma may see every entry she has made, regardless of which course it was in or whether she made it public or private.

- **Add a new entry**: Emma can choose to add a new blog entry here (as she could from her profile) which doesn't have to be specific to any particular course. If she sets it to "anyone on this site", then other users can read her blog wherever they are in Moodle.

- **Search**: At the bottom of the **Blog menu** block is a search box. This enables users to enter a word or phrase and see if anyone has mentioned it in a blog entry

The Recent Blog Entries block

As our teacher in the Beginners' French course Stuart has enabled the **Recent Blog Entries** block, there is also a block showing the latest blog entries. Emma's is the most recent entry on the course so hers appears as a link, along with all other recent course entries.

Course specific blogs

Just to recap and double check—if Emma now visits her other course, **How to Be Happy** and checks out the **View my entries about this course** entries link in the **Blog menu**, she does not see her French course blog post, but instead, sees an entry she has associated with this course:

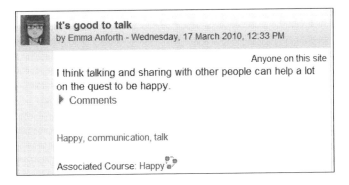

The tutor for this course, Andy, has added the blog tags block.

The blog tags block

This block is not new; however, it's worth pointing out that the tags are NOT course-specific, and so Emma sees the tags she added to the entries in both courses alongside the tags from other users:

Blog settings

So far we've just looked at how and where to add a blog entry. There are other settings connected to blogs which can be accessed from the profile **Settings** block (that is, *not* the navigation block). The following screenshot shows the path to the blog settings and it offers us three links:

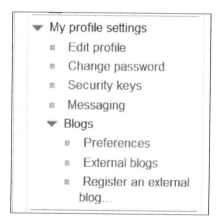

Preferences

This is where we can decide how many blog entries per page we'd like to see.

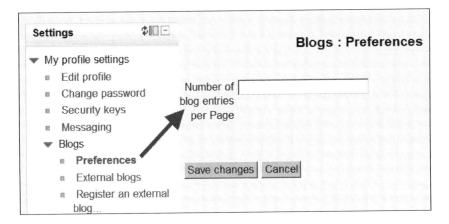

External blogs

A brand new feature for Moodle 2.0, this allows user's to bring external blog posts into Moodle by specifying the RSS/ATOM feed of the blog, which is then checked through a cron task and entries copied into the user's blog in Moodle. It could be a blog belonging to the user that they'd like to share within Moodle, or it could be the posts of an admired blogger that they'd like to display alongside their own blog posts. In the following example, Stuart, our French teacher has chosen to import the blog feeds of two online colleagues:

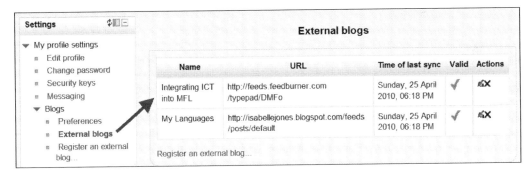

 The check in the **Valid** column tells us the feed is correctly set; the **Actions** column gives us the ability to edit or delete (*unregister*) an external blog. If no external blogs have been added then we simply see the link **Register an external blog**.

Register an external blog

Martin, our Moodle Manager would like to import into his Moodle blog the entries from a posterous blog he's been keeping over the last few months. To do so he has to take the following steps:

- He first needs to get the RSS feed of the blog he wants to register. In Martin's case, this is quite simple as he goes to his blog, looks for the orange RSS icon and grabs the feed URL from there. The next screenshot pinpoints where this is:

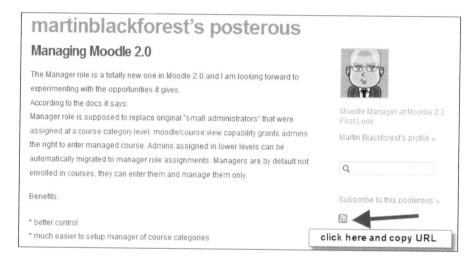

- He then clicks the **Register External blog** link we saw recently and fills in the relevant details:

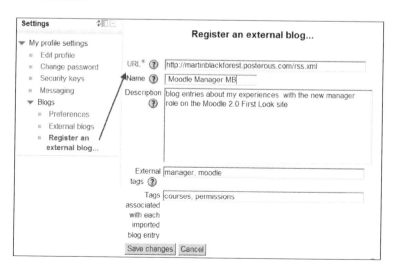

- He adds the information thus:
  - **URL**: The correct feed for the blog.
  - **Name**: A descriptive name (if left empty it will give the blog's actual name)
  - **Description**: A description of the contents (if left empty it will give the blog's actual description)
  - **External tags**: If tags entered here match those from blog posts then those blog posts will be copied in.
  - **Tags associated with each imported blog**: If the URL is correct, then when he clicks on the **Save changes** button, the following will appear and will be visible in the **External blogs** link.

External blogs

Name	URL	Time of last sync	Valid	Actions
Moodle Manager MB	http://martinblackforest.posterous.com /rss.xml	Saturday, 19 June 2010, 02.29 PM	✓	✎✗

- At the next cron job, the relevant entries will be copied over and Martin's blog will include entries from his posterous blog as well as his Moodle posts.

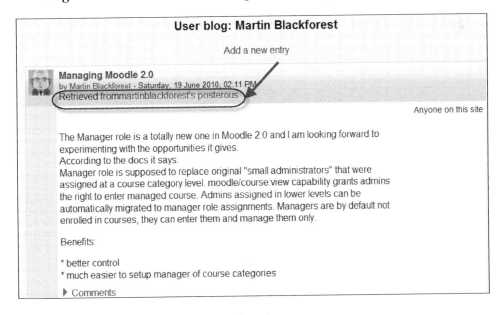

Admin issues

So far we've looked at blog entries from a student (Emma), teacher (Stuart and Andy) and manager's (Martin)point of view. But in order for the blogs to function as the managers, teachers and students wish, certain settings need to be enabled by the administrator. These include the following:

- Enabling (that is "opening the eye" of) the **Blog menu** block in **Site administration | plugins | blocks | manage blocks**

- Personalizing the blog settings in **Site administration | Appearance | blog**.

The final chapter of the book goes through the important admin settings in Moodle 2.0 and we will cover blog settings in more detail there.

Commenting on blogs

When Emma wrote her blog entries, we saw there was a link—**Comments**:

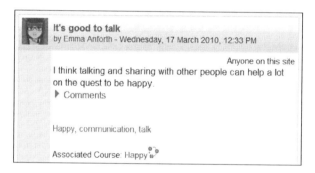

Clicking on the link brings up a box into which anyone (Emma included) can add a comment.

 You might see a whirring spiral when you click—it's the Ajax interface!

The teacher on the **How to be Happy** course, Andy, has entered a comment below and simply needs to click on **submit** for it to be registered.

When Emma returns to her blog entry and clicks on the **Comments** link, she sees a number—the number of comments—and can view any comments made. The commenter's name appears, so she if she has several comments she can see who said what. Below it is another empty box so she can add a response if she wishes.

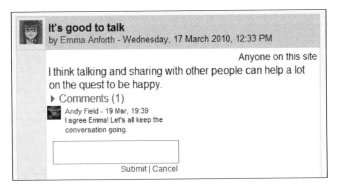

Getting a dialog going

In the past, Moodlers like ourselves have probably used forums to pass opinions back and forth. They still remain an excellent medium for discussion. However, now the ability to comment on blog entries opens up a better way of communicating within a course. A blog entry can have numerous comments attached to it, each with the user's name and time they commented. In the French course, we can see a conversation taking shape following Emma's first blog entry:

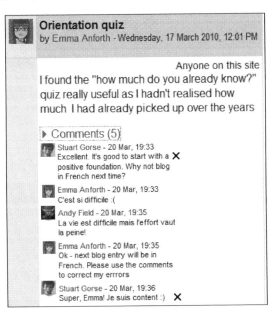

Deleting comments in a blog

A user can delete their own comments on any blog post, but not those of others. In the preceding screenshot, we are seeing Stuart's last comment—hence there is a cross (**X**) next to two of his posts.

The Moodle administrator has the power to delete all the comments if necessary and would have a cross (**X**), next to all of them.

Recap—the blog in Moodle 2.0

It is now possible in Moodle 2.0 to do the following:

- Have a blog associated with a course
- Have blog entries in several courses which are only seen in those courses
- Copy in external blog posts
- Comment on blog posts

Commenting on the Moodle blog is a bit of a workaround really; the Moodle blog doesn't really have a built-in commenting facility like, say Wordpress. Rather, Moodle is making use of the new **Comments** feature which ordinarily appears as a block anywhere you want to add it.

Let's now take a look at the possibilities this block brings us in Moodle 2.0.

Using the Comments block

As a teacher, adding a **Comments** block to the main course page is straightforward:

1. Turn on the editing.
2. Click the **Add a block** drop-down list.
3. Select **Comments**.

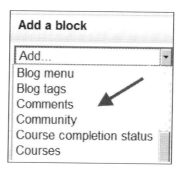

4. The **Comments** block appears.

5. Click on the configuration (hand/pen) icon to specify where exactly to position it:

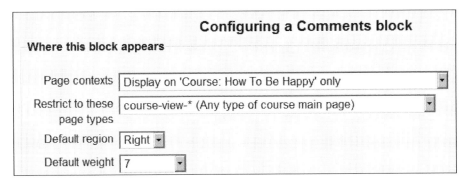

We saw in *Chapter 2, Finding our way around (Navigation and Blocks)*, how the new block handling system gives us far more control over the positioning of blocks in a course.

Any user of the course is able to type into the box and make a remark. Clicking on **Submit** (like with the blog) will send and save the comment. The following screenshot shows the *before* and *after* of adding a comment:

Deleting comments on the course page

The permissions here are slightly different from those inside a blog:

- A student can delete their own comments

- The teacher of the course can delete any/all of the comments

- The administrator can (of course) delete any/all of the comments

Why comment on the course page?

Our teacher in the Beginner's French course, Stuart, decided to add a **Comments** block to the main course page to get some feedback about the content of his course. As you can see from the next screenshot, using the block in this way provides a quick and easy method of viewing at a glance what people think of the course.

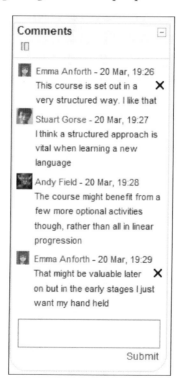

However, we've got the means to comment pretty much anywhere we want—so let's investigate some other places where commenting might be valuable!

What follows is not an exhaustive list, obviously, but just a few suggestions that might give you a few ideas for your own course.

Students comment on the usefulness of a resource

Andy, our teacher in the **How To Be Happy** course, has added several resources he feels the students might appreciate. Some are links to websites; others are downloadable resources. He would like the students to have a simple, one click way to let him know how useful the materials are to help him improve the course for future students.

An example is a PowerPoint he has added on **Top Ten Tips for a Good Night's Sleep**. When he uploaded it, in the editing screen, he set the **Display** option to **Embed**, as shown in the following screenshot:

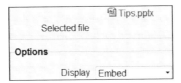

Once saved, this shows the link to the PowerPoint on its own page on the course—with the possibility to add a **Comments** block:

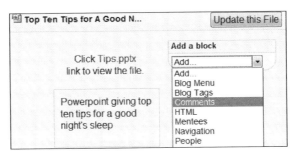

When he then clicks the configuration (hand/pen) icon, Andy gets the positioning options for this particular block. He chooses to have it showing only on this page where the link to the PowerPoint appears:

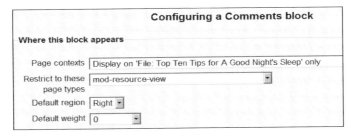

When a student such as Emma accesses this resource, she can now offer a comment as to its usefulness, and both Andy the teacher and any other students can see what she thinks:

 Note that the **X** is there because Andy as the teacher has the right to delete any comments on his course. Maybe if he changes his resource to a `.pdf` as she suggested, he might just do that..

Teachers comment in private (1)

By using the **assign roles** feature in a block, it's possible for Andy to enable any other teachers on his course to comment in private on aspects of the course.

What admin needs to do

For this to happen, the Moodle administrator needs to have given teachers the ability to override permissions in **Site Administration | Users | Permissions | Define Roles**.

From the **Allow role overrides** tab, the admin should enable the box enabling a **Teacher** (on the left) to override the roles of **Student** and **Authenticated user** —as shown in the following screenshot(a **Teacher** can already override the role of **Guest**):

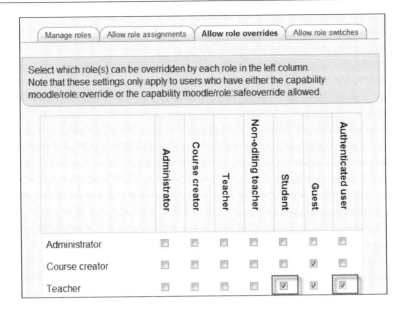

The following table shows the role overrides:

	Administrator	Course creator	Teacher	Non-editing teacher	Student	Guest	Authenticated user
Administrator	☐	☐	☐	☐	☐	☐	☐
Course creator	☐	☐	☐	☐	☐	☑	☐
Teacher	☐	☐	☐	☐	☑	☑	☑

This has risks attached—**Teachers** might grant or revoke the rights of others with undesired consequences.

What the teacher needs to do

In *Chapter 3, Editing text and managing files,* Andy sets up a **Happy Pics** assignment asking students to contribute a photograph of something that makes them happy. Andy would like a colleague with teacher permissions on the course to give feedback on its suitability as an assignment.

Clicking on it the assignment page with the editing turned on, again, Andy has the option to include a **Comments** block:

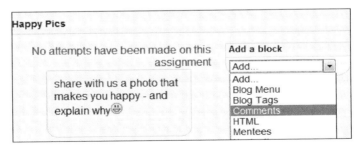

Then, when he clicks the configuration (hand/pen) icon, Andy gets the positioning options for this particular block. He selects to have it showing only on this assignment page:

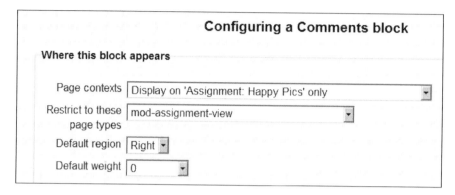

Once this is done, in order to hide the block from students and reveal it only to colleagues with the teacher permission, he needs to click on the assign roles icon as shown by the arrow in the following screenshot:

In the **Block Settings**, that then appears, Andy needs to select the **Permissions** and then click the **X** next to the **Student** and the **Authenticated user** to *prevent* anyone with the student role to view this block and be able to comment on the assignment:

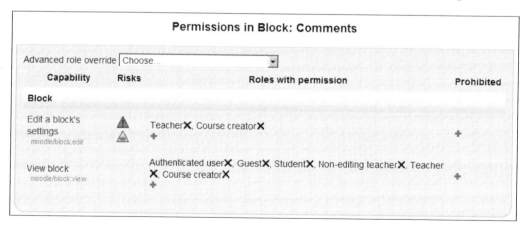

For each of these actions, a warning appears, just to make sure!

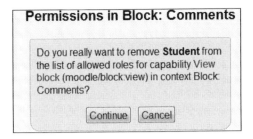

When Andy clicks on the **Continue** button, students are then no longer allowed to view this block. We can see this by comparing teacher Andy's view with student Emma's view of the assignment page, as shown in the following screenshot:

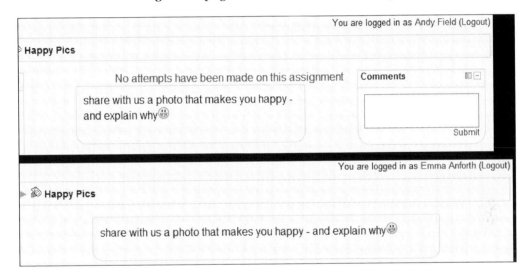

 We'll take a closer look at this new role/permissions interface in *Chapter 8, Admin Issues*

Teachers comment in private (2)

We just saw how using role overrides in a block can allow teachers to see comments that students can't. Another, simpler way to achieve this is to add a **Comments** block to a page that students wouldn't ordinarily see anyway; this way there are no issues with permissions.

Two teachers sharing a course could use a **Comments** block on the grading page of a particular assignment. This might be useful for moderation purposes—in the following example, Andy is concerned he might have marked too harshly. His teaching colleague can respond in the box while at the same time looking at the marks.

Moderating grades with a Comments block

To do this, Andy needs to do the following:

1. Turn on the editing
2. Click on the assignment he wishes to be moderated
3. Click the link **View submitted assignments**
4. On the next screen, add a **Comments** block in the way outlined before.

When this box is enabled, any editing teacher can see and add to it. Andy has begun to mark the assignment and is unsure about the grading. His colleague Martin comments:

It's not possible to comment in the grade book as a whole, just on individual assignments.

Students hold a dialogue during a workshop or Wiki

In collaborative activities such as wikis or workshops (which we looked at in *Chapter 5, What's new in Add an Activity*), the **Comments** block provides a useful way of allowing students to continue a conversation while still keeping an eye on the task at hand.

Moodle messaging or a Moodle forum can do this too, of course, but the former is private and the latter is separate from the actual exercise students are working together on.

In the following example, Andy has added a block to his **All you Need is Love** workshop (that we saw in *Chapter 5, What's new in Add an Activity*). As the workshop progresses through its various stages, students are able to comment as shown in the following screenshot:

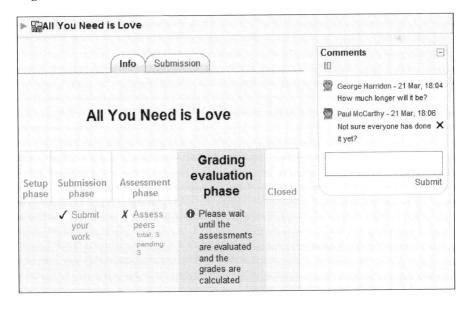

Recap—the Comments block in Moodle 2.0

We've seen how thoughtful use of the **Comments** block in Moodle 2.0 opens up communication channels between:

- Teachers and teachers privately
- Teachers and students
- Students and students

There are many pages which may be enhanced by the addition of a **Comments** block—it's well worth experimenting!

Moodle messaging

In this section on *Having your Say*, we'll take a look at the changes made to Moodle's messaging system.

What does admin need to do?

Moodle 2.0 messaging has to be turned on from **Site Administration | Advanced Features**.

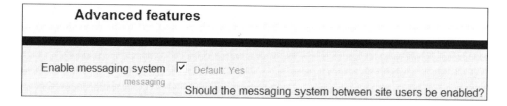

Where are my message options?

For any user of Moodle, the options for messaging can be accessed by clicking on the **My profile settings** which appear on the front page once logged in and in every course. As we saw in *Chapter 2, Finding our way around (Navigation and Blocks)*, the block can be expanded or condensed. Beginners' French teacher Stuart sees his **My profile settings** as follows:

Clicking on the blue **Messaging** link will bring up all the options; he has to configure them to his own preferences.

A site administrator, a course teacher, and a student all have slightly different versions of the messaging screen, so let's go through them one at a time:

What does admin see?

Admin's messaging preferences include site-wide concerns:

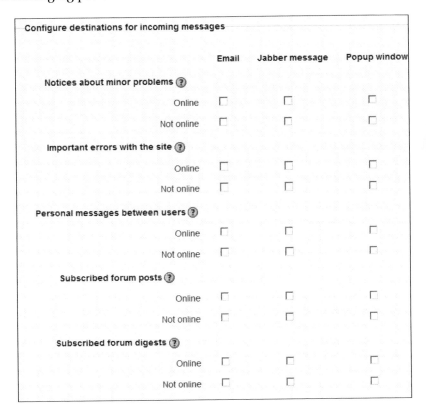

More messaging channels can be added as plug-ins;
for example, SMS messaging

There is the option to choose individually how each alert reaches admin. The
defaults are as follows:

- **Online**—Moodle messaging pop-up window
- **Not online**—e-mail

However, should your establishment use the messaging system **Jabber**, then it's also
possible to send a selected type of alert to this instead.

For example—I as an admin, might not be online on Moodle all day but if an
Important error with the site occurs, a message using Jabber could get to me more
quickly than Moodle messaging or e-mail. On the other hand, if it involves less
urgent **Notices about minor problems**, I could safely access them using a pop-up
if I happen to be using Moodle or through my e-mail later in the day.

Below the alert options are the sections where I tell Moodle my preferred **Email
address**, my **Jabber ID** and how I want pop-up messages to appear.

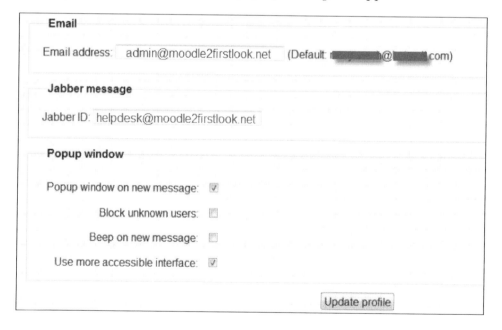

What does a teacher or student see?

While the Moodle admin has messaging options specific to their site wide role, other users—teachers and students—just have the final three options, as we can see in teacher Stuart's messaging setup screen in the following screenshot:

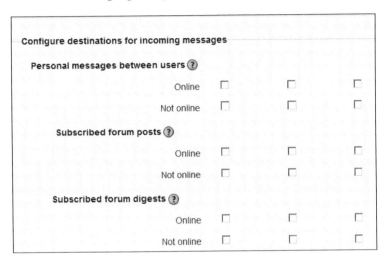

Other settings (such as e-mail, Jabber ID, pop-up preferences) are the same as for admin.

You can search for, add and manage contacts by clicking on the **Messages** link in the **Messages** block itself:

How do messages display?

Messages received no longer arrive in a pop-up window. Instead, they appear at the bottom right of your screen. You can choose to ignore it or click the link to read the message. The following screenshot shows the new-look messaging:

Giving feedback

As if being able to blog, comment, and message wasn't enough, Moodle 2.0 also gives us the option to add feedback instances both to our courses and to the site as a whole. The **Feedback** module isn't new; it's been around and popular for a while. Eventually it will combine with the equally popular **Questionnaire** module to make a turbo-charged feedback/survey/questionnaire, but in the meantime, the **Feedback** module has been added to Moodle 2.0 (although admins will need to "open its eye" to enable it)

Additionally, if we want to be able to get anonymous feedback on our home page—that is from non-logged in users, then admin needs to change to **Yes** the option in **Site administration | Plugins | Feedback** as shown in the following screenshot:

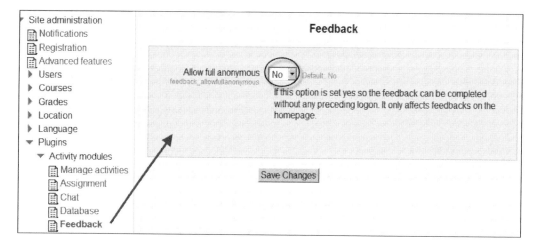

Why anonymous?

It's not so much that we don't want to know "who said what"—rather this way, we can create a short set of questions on the front page which people without a login are able to answer. At my school, we've used the Feedback module in Moodle 1.9 to survey students' parents on uniform preferences, and to query site visitors on what type of resources they would like to see in our Student Showcase. Business and Enterprise, students have used feedback as part of their research when assessing the potential demand for a product they wish to market. In commercial Moodles, Feedback can serve as a means to gauge the requirements of potential paying clients. Here on our *Moodle 2.0 First Look* site, our manager, Martin is going to add a feedback instance to the front page. If you've used **Feedback** in earlier versions of Moodle, there won't be much new to you here.

Adding a new feedback

With the editing turned on, Martin must do the following:

1. Click the **Add an Activity** drop-down menu and select **Feedback**.

2. Fill in the **Name**, **Description**, and Time settings (if needed) as shown in the following screenshot:

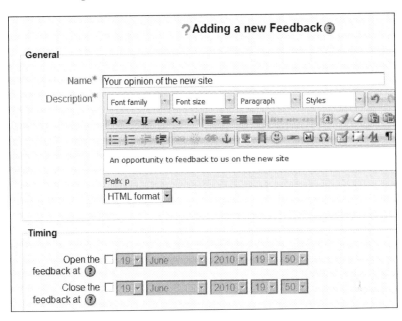

3. Decide upon the **Feedback options** as shown in the following screenshot:

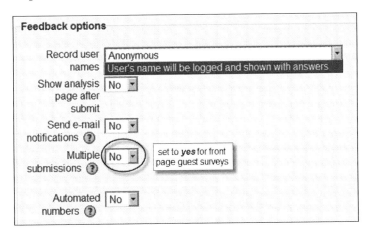

- **Record user names**: This is where to decide whether to have anonymous feedback or not.

- **Show analysis page after submit**: If this is set to **Yes**, users will see the results so far.

- **Send e-mail notifications**: If this is set to **Yes**, administrators will get notification of feedback responses.

- **Multiple submissions**: If this is set to **Yes** for anonymous surveys then many people can submit feedback (or one user can submit feedback many times!) Martin needs to set his to **Yes.**

- **Automated numbers**: If this is set to **Yes**, Moodle will number the questions automatically.

Martin must then perform the following:

1. Choose a post-survey thankyou message or web address to redirect users once they've given feedback:

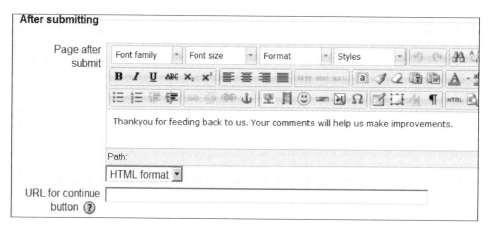

2. Decide on the **Common Module settings** and **Availability** along with other activities.

3. Click on **Save and Display** to bring up the editing screen as shown in the following screenshot:

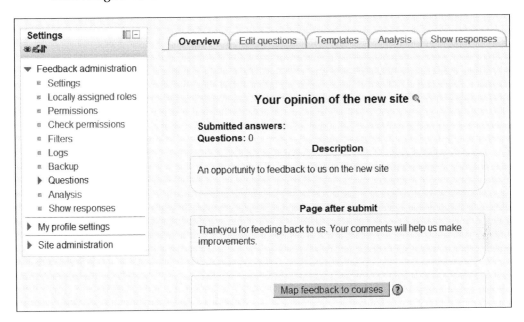

- **Edit questions**: This is where Martin can choose a question type for his first question. The choices appear in a drop-down:

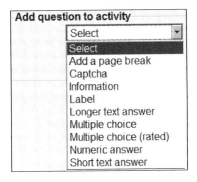

- **Templates**: Previously set up questions can be saved as a template, or Martin can save the current questions as a new template for future use.

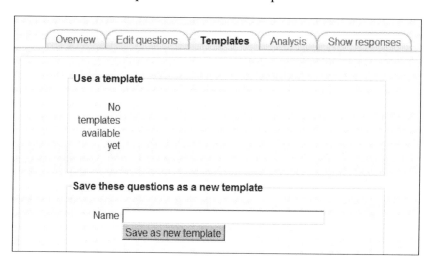

- **Analysis**: Here's where the results are analyzed! Note in the following screenshot the ability to export the results to Excel if desired.

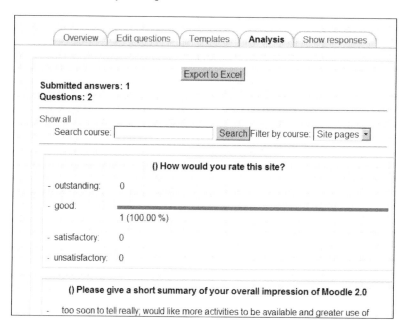

- **Show responses**: Clicking on the **Course analysis (Submitted answers)** link will take us and Martin to the individual responses in this feedback survey. Note that as it is a front page anonymous survey we get the message **No existing students**. Even if a logged in user such as Emma completes the survey, her response will be shown as anonymous here.

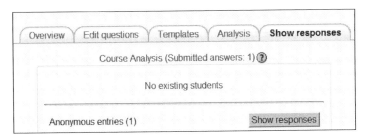

Giving feedback

Finally, having seen how Martin set it up, it's important to see the activity from a user's point of view. If we return to our front page we see the feedback with its own icon—with this theme, a Question mark:

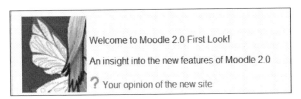

Clicking on the link brings us to an introductory screen where we are prompted to **Answer the questions**, as the following screenshot shows:

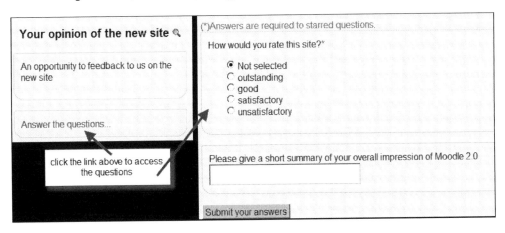

Summary

In this chapter, we've concerned ourselves with *Having your Say* – new ways in Moodle 2.0 to get our message across, communicate with other users. We've looked at:

- Blogs: How they can be more easily used in courses and with comments
- The Comments block: How it enables you to voice your opinions almost anywhere in Moodle
- Messaging: How you now have more control over different types of alert
- Feedback: Not new, but included as an option in Moodle 2.0

So far we have just looked briefly at administration issues as we've come across them. *Chapter 8, Admin issues* will go into more detail about the changes and improvements to administration in Moodle 2.0.

8
Admin Issues

This chapter takes a look at Moodle 2.0 from the administrator's point of view. It's not an exhaustive study; rather, it focuses on the principal areas where Moodle 2.0 differs from previous versions. If you want a detailed and fully comprehensive manual, Alex Büchner's Moodle Administration, also published by Packt and updated for Moodle 2.0, will be a useful addition to your Moodle library.

The navigation block

As we saw in an earlier chapter, when you first visit a Moodle 2.0 site you see a **Navigation** block with a link to the courses, plus any other items you might have on your front page.

When you log in, this block offers four links, which expand to different options according to your permissions:

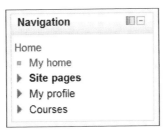

- **My home**: This is a link to a user's personalized **MyMoodle** page. We'll see later in **Appearance** how you can make the user's front page default to **MyMoodle** and instead have this as the link to the site home page.

- **Site pages**: This expands to show site pages such as blogs or tags. Depending on the user's permissions they might also see **Reports** and/or **Participants**. See the difference between admin's view and our student Emma's view in the following screenshot:

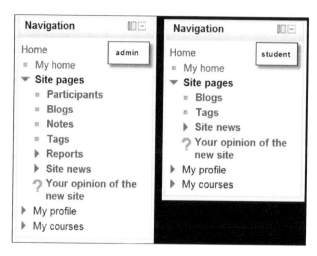

- **My profile**: This gives the user quick access to their profile, blogs, and messages. Again, users with extra permissions will have extra links such as **Notes** and **Activity Reports**. If you want to edit aspects of your profile, this is done with a link in the separate **Settings** block. The following screenshot shows student Emma's view. As she has no other front page or site permissions, the **Settings** block only allows her to edit her profile:

Other users with greater permissions will have more links in their **Settings** block as we shall see in a moment.

- **My courses**: Clicking this link will display the user's courses.

The Settings block

Once logged in, Moodle gives us a **Settings** block providing access to various features according to our permissions. This block remains with us throughout our journey through the site. This is useful for admin, for example, as they could access **Site administration** options when inside a course, rather than having to go back to the front page.

We saw that students like Emma only have one option in their **Settings** block—the ability to edit their profile (if we want them to).

A user with a front page role, like our manager Martin, will also have a link to **My profile settings**. Additionally, he will have a link to **Front page settings** as shown in the following screenshot. He will also see a **Site administration** link. However, this merely leads to more **Front page** settings, as this is the only site administration capability he has.

An administrator, of course, has **Front page settings**, **My profile settings**, and the full range of **Site administration** options as we see in the following screenshot:

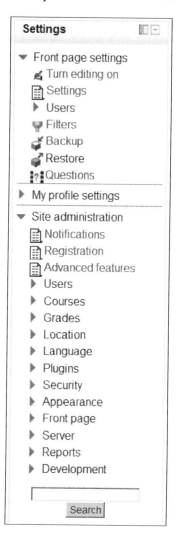

This chapter will take a dual approach to administration in Moodle 2.0:

- We'll go through those **Site administration** options to see what's new for a Moodle admin.

- Then we'll take a look at how a teacher handles administration within their course.

Changes in Site administration

Perhaps the simplest way to explore this is to look at how this menu has altered since Moodle 1.9:

Notifications/Registrations

A small but important change in Moodle 1.9, the **Notifications** screen contained a button you could click to register your site with `http://moodle.org/`. The page this took you to now has its own billing in Moodle 2.0, as the **Registration** link.

Community hubs

The main Moodle community hub is known as **MOOCH** and you register with it here. You can also register your site with other community hubs.

Register your site	
Moodle.org	**Specific hub**
The main community hub is called MOOCH, at hub.moodle.org. By registering your site with MOOCH you will contribute to the statistics of the worldwide Moodle community. You can also join a low-volume mailing list providing early notifications of security fixes and new releases of Moodle.	You can also register your site with other community hubs.
Register with Moodle.org now	Register with a specific hub

Registered with	
Hub	**Actions**
Moodle.org	Unregister

If you register with hubs, then teachers can add a **Community** block in their courses where users can search for a suitable course to enrol in or download.

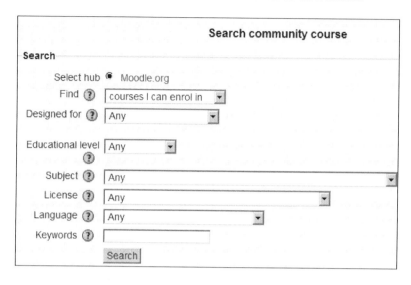

This is a very powerful new feature of Moodle 2.0 and should be widely encouraged combining the true spirit of Open Source and educators sharing resources.

Advanced features

Some features of Moodle will not necessarily be needed by everyone and could indeed clutter up the administration menu. The **Advanced features** link gathers together these and enables administrators to choose the ones their site will need, and ignore the others. Some options such as enabling outcomes and notes are not new to Moodle but others, such as, enabling comments, portfolios, and web services are.

While it's useful to note that **Advanced features** is the screen where features such as portfolios or web services may be enabled, we will actually study the consequences in the appropriate section of **Site administration**.

 Note that, if you want to enable **RSS feeds** in Moodle 2.0, here's where you do it! Formerly you'd have gone to the **Server** section of **Site administration** to check the **enable RSS feeds** box.

Towards the bottom of the list, we find the settings to turn networking on or off and those for **Completion tracking** and **Conditional Availability** discussed in *Chapter 6, Managing the Learning Path.*

Completion tracking

If this is enabled, then teachers of courses can decide within their own settings whether to use it and have their students see a check after each activity which displays progress through a course.

Progress tracked roles

Any roles selected here will see the checks against activities. Traditionally, this would be students in a course.

Enable conditional availability

This is the setting which, when selected globally here, will allow individual teachers like our *Beginners' French* tutor Stuart to set up Conditional Activities as seen in *Chapter 6, Managing the Learning Path*.

What's new in Users

Let's move on to the **Users** link now:

Authentication

Well, if you are used to Moodle 1.9 and you are expecting to manage authentication via **Site administration | Users | Authentication**, you will be confused and disappointed! The **Authentication** link has been moved to **Plugins**, so we'll check it out there.

Bulk User Actions

New here is the ability to bulk enrol users into a course directly from the users list. We can select users as before in **Bulk User Actions** and in the drop down choose **Enrol the users**.

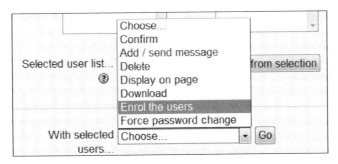

Clicking on **Go** button then takes us to a screen where our selected users are listed against available courses. The boxes are checked if the users are already enrolled in a course. If we want to enrol them into a new course, we simply check the empty box.

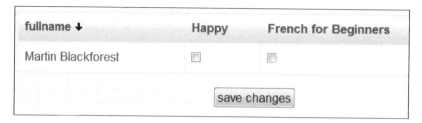

Cohorts

This is Moodle 2.0's take on the long wished for site-wide groups. When we click on the link we're taken to the following screen where we click on **Add** to enter details of the **cohort** we want to create:

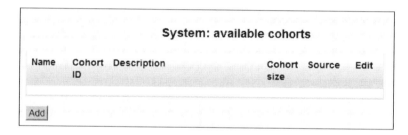

In the screen that comes up next, it's useful to note that we can make a **System** cohort (that is, we can select this group in any course site-wide) or a cohort that applies only to one category. Our Moodle 2.0 currently only has the **Miscellaneous** category available so it's the only other option.

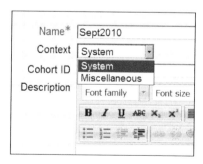

Once the details have been completed and saved, we're returned to the initial screen (**1** in the following screenshot) where we see our cohort is available, but currently has no members. Clicking on **Assign** will allow us to choose from users on our Moodle whom we can manually add to this cohort (**2** in the following screenshot).

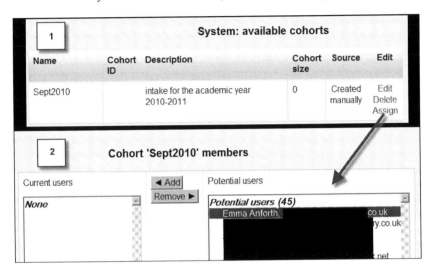

We'll look at how to add a cohort to a course later on, in the section on *Course administration*.

Permissions

The **Permissions** settings have been enhanced in Moodle 2.0. Let's go through the additions:

User Policies

When selecting users to assign roles to or add to a group, we can now search and display them by:

- **Email address**
- **ID number**
- **Username**(although this is not recommended for security reasons)

Additionally, the setting in **User Policies** of Moodle 1.9 to **Allow users without the assign roles capability to switch roles** is not present in Moodle 2.0 as it is dealt with elsewhere.

Site administrators

This is a new link which allows us to select and manage the site administrators. It's in a page of its own, unlike in previous versions of Moodle where it was possible to select administrators from the **Assign System roles** screen. This is to help prevent issues with users being inappropriately assigned an administrator role and also to prevent system roles being misused. It is now no longer possible to remove from the list the primary administrator once more, to avoid previous disasters with newbie administrators mistakenly deleting themselves from their own Moodle.

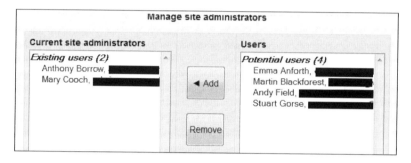

Define roles

We see here in the following screenshot, the new role of manager and the simplified way we can edit them from the column far right. In addition to the pen/hand edit icon allowing us to adjust the role and the **X** allowing us to delete it, the **x2** allows us to create a new role based on this particular role.

The **new-to-2.0** tab in **Allow role switches** is where we can select who can switch roles to whom, provided they have the `moodle/role:switchroles` capability.

Assign system roles

In earlier versions of Moodle, this was where the administrator could assign roles to users, which they retained throughout the whole Moodle site. Indeed, there was a prominent warning alerting administrators to the possible repercussions of doing so. Despite the warning, students or teachers were often assigned globally and then failed to understand why they could access all courses. This and other associated problems with global role assignments made it evident that system roles had to be reevaluated. Now, when we go to the screen in Moodle 2.0 we see the following:

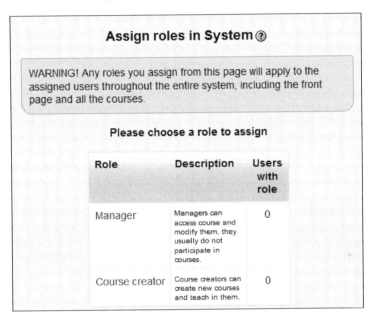

While the warning is still present, the only roles we can assign globally from here are the **Manager** role and **Course creator** role, both of which make sense to be assigned everywhere in Moodle. It is simply no longer possible to have your students appear site wide throughout your Moodle because they have been assigned from this **Assign roles in System** screen.

Check system permissions

We can use this feature to check the permissions and permission overrides of anyone on our Moodle, and ensure they are only allowed to do what is appropriate and intended for them. As an example, if we select our student Emma and then click on **Show this user's permissions**. We see from the very first items in the following list that (quite naturally) she doesn't have the capability to upload users but is allowed to make blog entries. What is allowed and what is not allowed are in different colors. In my current theme, for example, they would be green and pink respectively.

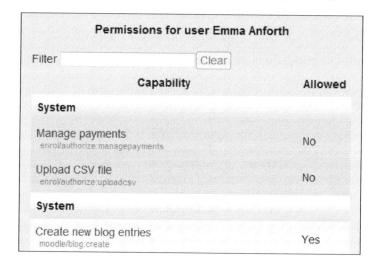

Capability reports

Following on from this in the **Users** list, is a screen where we can check precisely which role has which capability in our Moodle. A couple of examples might make this clearer. Let's check if the new role of manager is allowed to delete comments. We select the **Delete comments** capability in the list, select **Manager** from the roles and then click on **Get the report**.

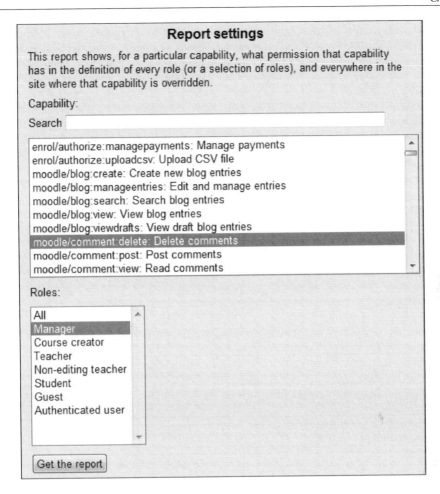

We then see that a Moodle Manager does have this capability:

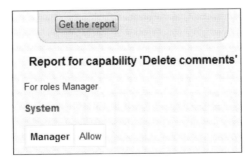

In another example, let's investigate how easy it is to check on altered permissions, adapted roles. Under normal circumstances, students should not be able to view hidden course categories, and if we look at all the roles, we see that this is the case. Managers and course creators are able to view them, but for other users it is not set.

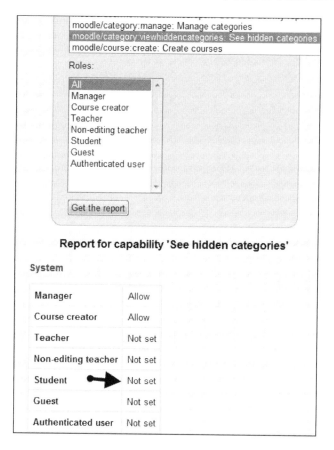

However, we can change that by going to **Define Roles**, selecting **Student**, clicking on the edit icon and checking the **Allow** box:

Notice how much clearer the interface is for editing roles in Moodle 2.0!

Now if we run the **Capability Report** again, we learn that students are now able to view hidden categories:

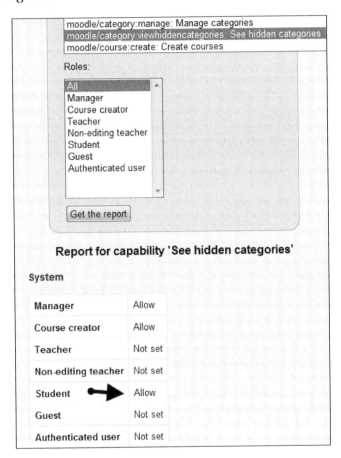

This is going to be a real boon to help resolve all those confusing and complex *who can do what?* issues in Moodle !

What's new in Courses

While we're leaving the individual course administration till later on in this chapter, it's useful to note here the increased options in **Course default settings**.

It's been possible for several versions of Moodle to set as default certain features when new courses are created, for example, whether to have **Topics** or **Weekly** format or whether to show the **News** forum or not. Moodle 2.0 takes this one step further by giving us the opportunity on this screen to decide globally on enrolment, groups, availability, and language—items which previously could only be done on an individual course basis. Thus, we could force groups in all activities in all our courses, or we could set a default enrolment key. These settings may of course be changed by the teachers in each course, but as institutions often have certain policies to ensure consistency across courses, having more default options is an advantage and time saver.

What's new in Grades

If you have JavaScript switched on then you can now enable AJAX in **Report settings | Grader Report**:

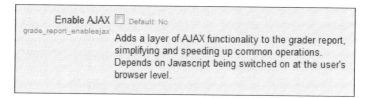

What's new in Location

If you want to specify a list of countries that may be selected from your Moodle, in a user's profile, for example, then you can do so in **Location Settings**. Leaving the setting blank simply means that the standard countries list will be used.

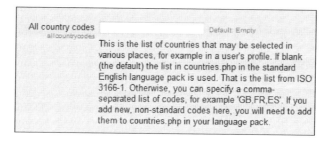

What's new in Plugins

The **Plugins** menu is, in fact, completely new in Moodle 2.0, although it incorporates elements located elsewhere in earlier versions of Moodle. Let's take each item one at a time:

Activity modules

This link is the Moodle 2.0 equivalent to **Modules | activities** in Moodle 1.9. When expanded, it displays the settings pages for the activity modules. New here are:

- **File**: Defaults for displaying a resource (has elements of the old **Resource** link).
- **Folder**: Options for displaying a folder (formerly known as **directory!**).
- **Page**: Defaults for displaying this page (has elements of the old **webpage/text page**).
- **URL**: Defaults for displaying links to websites (previously included in **Resource**).

Blocks

This equates to the **Blocks** link in Moodle 1.9 although we have lost **sticky blocks** now, as the new way of handling blocks lets us to make blocks sticky pretty much anywhere we want. New here is:

- **Tags**: An option to show (or not) the course tagging features in the **Tags** block, allowing students to tag courses.

Authentication

Formerly in **Site administration | Users**, this has moved to the **Plugins** link. New in the authentication plugins are **Web Services**, which, as we just saw, could be enabled in **Advanced Features**.

Active authentication plugins			
Name	Enable	Up/Down	Settings
Manual accounts			Settings
No login			Settings
Web services authentication	👁	↓	Settings

Clicking on the blue **Settings** link gives us the message: **This authentication method should be used for accounts that are exclusively for use by webservice client**. We will see more about **Web services** later.

Enrolments

Formerly a part of the **Courses** link, this has now been significantly revamped with much more flexibility now. The old enrolment plugins have been rewritten. Course enrolment information is stored in a separate database table `user_enrolments` and we can use SQL to find enrolled users in any course extremely quickly.

Manage enrol plugins

Clicking here brings up the following screen. If we "open the eye" of any disabled plugins they are then available as links in this section.

Available course enrolment plugins

Name	Instances / enrolments	Enable	Up/Down	Settings	Uninstall
Manual enrolments	6 / 11	👁	↓	Settings	Uninstall
Guest access	4 / 0	👁	↑ ↓	Settings	Uninstall
Self enrolment	5 / 1	👁	↑ ↓	Settings	Uninstall
Cohort sync	2 / 8	👁	↑	Settings	Uninstall
Category enrolments	0 / 0	👁		Settings	Uninstall
External database	0 / 0	👁		Settings	Uninstall
Flat file (CSV)	0 / 0	👁		Settings	Uninstall
IMS Enterprise file	0 / 0	👁		Settings	Uninstall
LDAP enrolments	0 / 0	👁		Settings	Uninstall
Course meta link	0 / 0	👁		Settings	Uninstall
MNet remote enrolments	0 / 0	👁		Settings	Uninstall
PayPal	0 / 0	👁		Settings	Uninstall

Let's take a look at the new ones:

- **Manual enrolments**: This plugin should be enabled by default, as it allows users to be enrolled manually by teachers using a link in the course administration settings. The enrolment period and default role may be set here.

- **Guest access**: We can specify the settings for guest access in a course here, for example, whether we want a password, a password hint, or whether we wish to allow temporary guest access by default.

- **Self enrolment**: This requires the **manual enrolment** plugin to be enabled in the course too and allows users to choose which courses they wish to participate in. We require an enrolment key in all new courses. Choose to send a welcome message or not, use group enrolment keys by default, and again set the enrolment period and default user (usually student, of course).

- **Cohort sync**: The **cohort enrolment** plugin synchronizes cohort members with course participants.

- **Category enrolments**: This has its eye closed by default and is actually a legacy solution for enrolments at the course category level via role assignments. Course category enrolments via role assignments are no longer possible. If you are enrolling from new, use cohort synchronization instead.

- **Course meta link**: This plugin synchronizes enrolments and roles in two different courses. By default, all course-level role assignments are synchronized from parent to child courses but here you can select roles which will not be synchronized and the current roles will be updated with the next cron job.

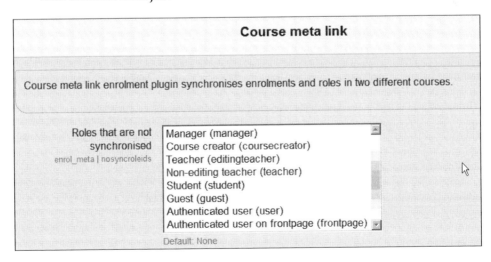

Text editors

This is where we can access settings for the new TinyMCE editor. In Moodle 1.9 its previous incarnation, was located in **Appearance | HTML editor**. We can choose to disable it here and we can also select our preferred spell engine.

License

We can set the default site license and manage the licenses (Public Domain/ARR/CCSA and so on) for our Moodle site here, choosing to display all of them as options when files are uploaded, or else to select only the ones relevant to our establishment.

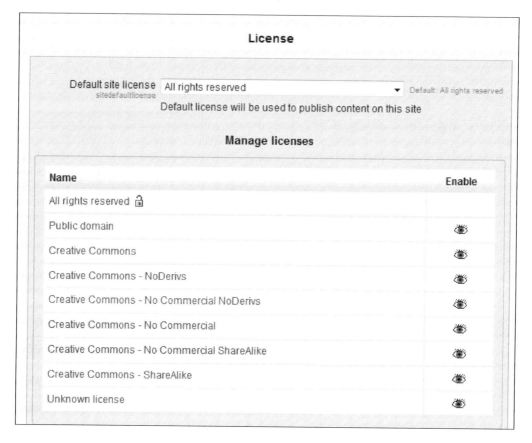

If you need to know more about the implications of each license, the following link from the Creative Commons website should be useful: `http://creativecommons.org/about/licenses/`.

Filters

This equates to the **Filters** menu in Moodle 1.9. However, we have far more control over where filters are enabled. The **Manage Filters** screen in Moodle 2.0 looks like the following screenshot (note—the screenshot only displays the first three filters):

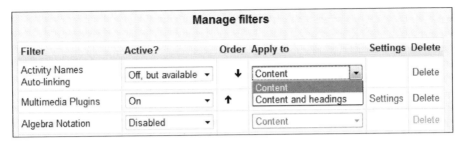

Previously, filters were either **On** or **Off**. Now we have three choices:

- **Disabled**: Nobody, in any course, can enable a filter.
- **On**: A filter is enabled by default and teachers can disable if they wish to.
- **Off but available**: A filter is off but teachers can enable it in their own courses.

Once a filter is enabled or made optionally available, we can then choose to apply it either to the **Content** or to the **Content and headings**, bearing in mind of course that applying filters to headings as well as content can increase the load on the server.

Portfolios

If we checked the box in **Advanced Features** to enable portfolios, here's where we can configure and manage remote systems so our users can export content to them.

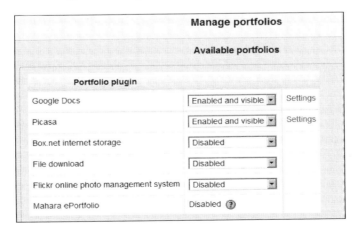

We've seen the practical applications of this in an earlier chapter.

Repositories

Brand new to Moodle 2 is where we can add and activate selected repository plugins for our users in their courses. The following screenshot shows only some of those available:

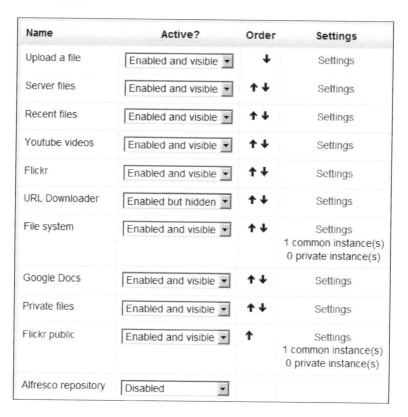

Name	Active?	Order	Settings
Upload a file	Enabled and visible	↓	Settings
Server files	Enabled and visible	↑ ↓	Settings
Recent files	Enabled and visible	↑ ↓	Settings
Youtube videos	Enabled and visible	↑ ↓	Settings
Flickr	Enabled and visible	↑ ↓	Settings
URL Downloader	Enabled but hidden	↑ ↓	Settings
File system	Enabled and visible	↑ ↓	Settings 1 common instance(s) 0 private instance(s)
Google Docs	Enabled and visible	↑ ↓	Settings
Private files	Enabled and visible	↑ ↓	Settings
Flickr public	Enabled and visible	↑	Settings 1 common instance(s) 0 private instance(s)
Alfresco repository	Disabled		

 It is advised to enable the **Course files repository** as this will make locating files easier for those users familiar with the previous course files structure

Repository example 1: Flickr

In the previous screenshot, **Flickr** has been set to **Enabled and visible**. On enabling this, a **Settings** screen appears for us to add the **Flickr API key** from our Flickr site in order to make the connection:

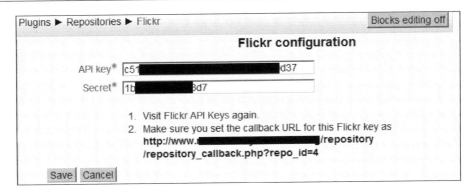

Repository example 2: File System—an FTP workaround

In earlier versions of Moodle, it was possible to FTP straight into a course directory if you knew its number. Site files for instance were always directory number 1. As we've seen, such a directory structure no longer exists but there's nothing preventing the Moodle admin from creating a folder on the server that permitted users to FTP and then adding it here. Here's how it's done:

1. Locate the `moodledata` folder on your server.

2. Inside it, locate the `repository` folder.

3. Inside it, create a new folder with a name of your choice.

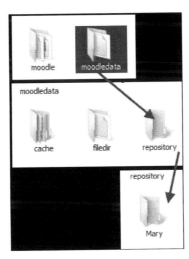

4. With **File System** set to **Enabled and visible**, click on **Settings**.

5. In the next screen, give permissions as desired.

6. Allow users to add a repository instance in the course.

7. Allow users to add a repository instance in the user context.

8. Scroll down and click on **Create a repository instance**.

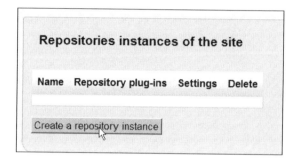

9. Select the folder you made and give it a name.

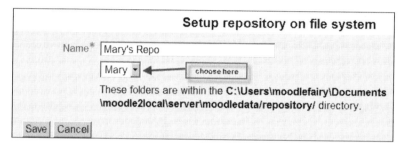

What does a course tutor see?

If a teacher such as Andy or Stuart accesses the file picker now he will have, alongside the other repositories, a link to the folder we just made and named:

Repository example 3: Webdav—another FTP workaround

If you're familiar with Webdav as an alternative to FTP, this is available in **Repositories** too. As with the others:

1. Set it to **Enabled and visible** and click on **Settings**.

2. Choose your configuration options as before.

3. Click **Create a repository instance**.

4. In the screen that appears, add your webdav details:

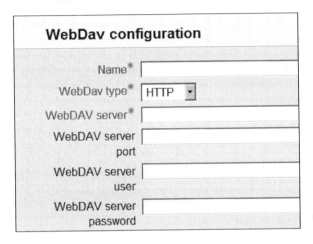

Also in **Manage Repositories** are:

- **Cache expire**: A box letting us choose the cache expire time when browsing repositories

- **Allow external links:** A checkbox allowing users to choose whether or not links are copied into Moodle. If it is **Off** then media will be copied into Moodle by default.

Webservices

We've seen that **Webservices** can be enabled in **Advanced Features**; we also found **Webservices** in **Plugins | Authentication**.

Webservices apply to developers and system integrators. Typically, they are application programming interfaces (APIs) accessed via HTTP and executed on a remote system hosting the requested services. Here, we have the settings for this new facility in Moodle 2.0:

- **Overview**: This screen helps us set up the Moodle web service for one system controlling Moodle, such as a student information service, or for users as clients. It also takes us through setting up the recommended token (security key) authentication method.

- **External services**: This screen is where we can add a **Custom service**, as in the following screenshot. Clicking **Add** at the bottom of screenshot 1 on the left displays the **External service** details as in 2 on the right.

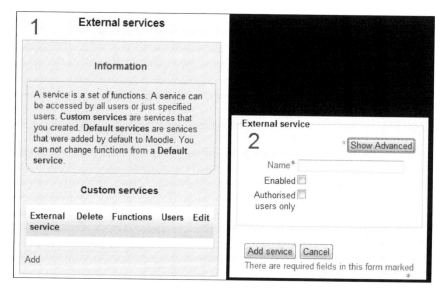

- **Manage protocols**: Here is where (if web services were enabled in **Advanced Features**) we can manage our active web service protocols and also, should we wish, give a web service user access to his own documentation without logging into Moodle.

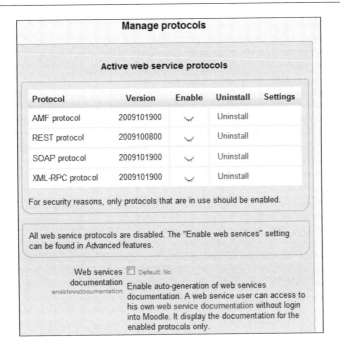

- **Manage tokens**: Here is where we can manage or add user tokens to particular web services. We can also include an IP restriction and set an end date.

Question types

Quiz question types can be viewed, disabled, or uninstalled here.

Question type	No. questions	Version	Requires	Available?	Delete	Settings
⋮≡ Multiple choice	1	2009021800		👁 ↑ ↓		
•• True/False	1	2006032200		👁 ↑ ↓		
▭ Short answer	1	2006032200		👁 ↑ ↓		
⦂?⦂ Random short-answer matching	0	2006042800	Short answer	👁 ↑ ↓	Delete	
2+2 =? Calculated	0	2010020800	Numerical	👁 ↑ ↓	Delete	

Manage question types

Local plugins

This is where you can view and manage any local plugins, that is, locally customized plugins with their own database, versions, strings, and so on.

What's new in security

Let's take a look at that most essential aspect of any Learning Management system—security.

IP blocker

In Moodle 2.0 it is possible to block users (or allow them) based on their IP address. By default, blocked IPs will be processed first unless you check the **Allowed** box. It also supports wildcards, for example *.ac.uk.

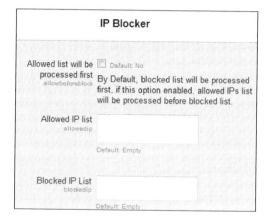

Site policies

It is possible to select the roles that are visible on user profile and participants' pages. The default is as below:

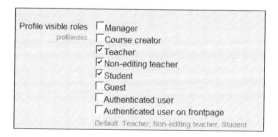

What's new in appearance

There have been some quite significant changes in the way Moodle looks, as we've seen so far in this book. We'll begin with **Themes:**

Themes

The themes structure has been completely rewritten for Moodle 2.0. Themes that worked in 1.9 needed to be updated to work in 2.0. There is a wide variety of attractive new themes available. If you need to update your own theme or would like information on Moodle 2.0 theming, you will find the documentation at `http://docs.moodle.org/en/Development:Themes_2.0` helpful

Theme settings

New to Moodle 2.0 are the following:

- **Designer Mode**: Turn this on so you're not served cached versions of themes, if you are designing themes or developing code.
- **Allow theme changes in the URL**: Enabling this will let users alter their theme via their Moodle URL using the syntax
- **Allow blocks to use the dock**: Enabling this will allow users to dock blocks if the theme supports it.

Individual theme settings pages

Moodle 2.0 theme developers can choose to include an individual theme settings page for their theme which will allow an administrator to customize the theme by, for example, changing its background color, adding a logo, and so on.

 If you're interested in this then take a look at the Moodle docs at `http://docs.moodle.org/en/Development:Themes_2.0_ adding_a_settings_page`

In the following screenshot, we have examples of such theme settings pages:

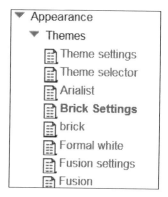

If we take a look at the **Brick Settings** link, this is what we come across first:

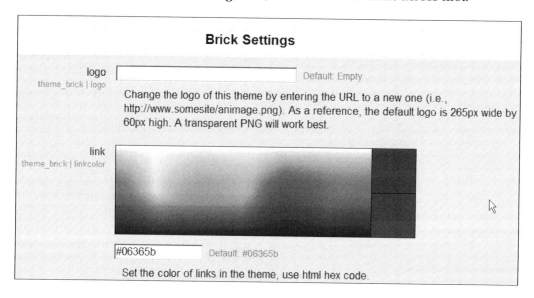

We've got the ability to change the logo and to set the color of the links using either a color picker or code. Scrolling further down gives us the opportunity to change the menu bar and block title's color, the heading color, and more. Magic! And that's only one theme.

Blog

New to the **Appearance** list are the settings for **Blogs**. We can:

- **Enable blog associations**: Allow blog entries to be associated with courses
- **Blog visibility**: Control and disable the viewing of blogs
- **Enable external blogs**: Allow users to add links to blogs outside of Moodle
- **External blog cron schedule**: Decide how often Moodle will check for new external blog entries
- **Maximum number of external blogs per user**: Set how many external blogs a user can link to
- **Enable comments**: Comments may be enabled or disabled here
- **Show comments count**: This will display the number of comments

Navigation

Here we can tweak the navigation in several ways:

- Decide the default home page for users or allow them to choose their own:

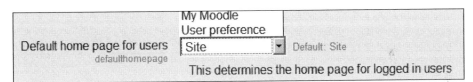

- Show or hide the course categories by default in the navigation bar and blocks
- Show or hide other courses in the navigation when a user is in one particular course
- Show all courses in the navigation at all times

Default MyMoodle page

Here we can customize the default **MyMoodle** page. It's worth noting that on the **MyMoodle** page we can add blocks to the middle as well as the sides. With editing turned on, we're given the option to move a block to a central location.

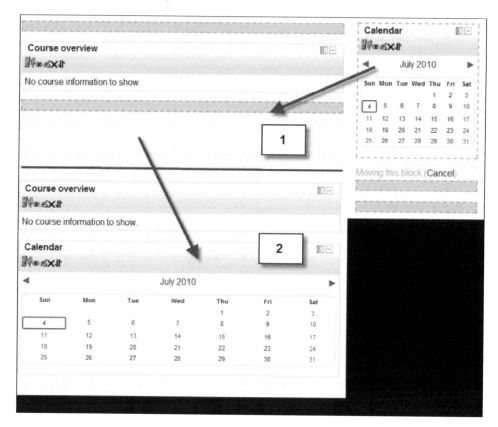

Default profile page

We can customize this too, and, as with the **MyMoodle** page, may also move blocks to a central position.

Course Contacts

Formerly known as **Course managers**, this is where we select who appears in the description of the course. It, now of course, includes the **Manager** role.

Ajax and JavaScript

In addition to enabling and disabling Ajax from this screen, we can also choose from here to use online YUI libraries and to enable/disable YUI combo loading.

What's new in Front page

Let's take a look at the differences in Front page administration.

Front page settings

One additional option here is the ability to select how many comments to be displayed on each page.

Users

This expands to:

Groups

Here we can define groups we want for the **Front Page**.

Permissions

Selecting **Permissions** takes us to a screen where we can see which roles have which capabilities on the front page. To remove a capability from them we just have to click on the **X** next to a role. To prohibit fully, a more drastic measure, we click the **+** under **Prohibit**. In the following screenshot, if users are given a Manager role on the front page, we can prevent them viewing live logs.

Capability	Risks	Roles with permission	Prohibited
Course report: Course completion			
View course completion report coursereport/completion:view	⚠	Non-editing teacher**X**, Teacher**X**, Manager**X** **+**	**+**
Course report: Live logs			
View course logs coursereport/log:view	⚠	Non-editing teacher**X**, Teacher**X**, Manager**X** **+**	**+**
View live logs coursereport/log:viewlive	⚠	Non-editing teacher**X**, Teacher**X**, Manager**X**	click to prevent
View today's logs coursereport/log:viewtoday	⚠	Non-editing teacher**X**, Teacher**X**, Manager**X** **+**	**+**

Front page roles

We can see the following differences:

- Roles have been rationalized: There is no need for administrators, guests, or Course Creators to have a front page role, so Moodle 2.0 doesn't list them

- A new role, Manager, is available, in response to popular requests for a non-visible course administrative assistant. (It's available throughout Moodle of course, not just here)

Front page filters

We've seen that Moodle has filters which the site administrator can enable or disable in **Plugins | Filters**. However, what is new and a significant improvement is that the filters can be disabled locally such as on the **Front Page** or in individual courses, provided they are enabled initially. On our **Front Page** we see that multimedia filters have been enabled globally. We could therefore choose to retain this setting or disable it.

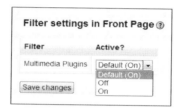

Also, it's possible for admin to set filters to be **Off but available** giving teachers in their own areas of Moodle, the possibility of enabling filters, if they wish to. We see in the following screenshot that **Activity Names Auto-linking** has been set to **Off but available** globally, giving us the option on the **Front Page** to turn it on.

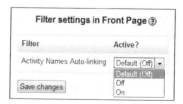

Front Page backup/restore

These work in a similar way to course backup and restore which we'll explore in our *Course Administration* section shortly.

Where are site files?

In Moodle 1.9 the front page menu gave us a link to so-called **Site files**. Anything uploaded here was publicly accessible without a login. It was possible (although, rather inadvisable and insecure) to add materials to the site files and then link to them from several courses, rather than having to duplicate those same resources a number of times.

With the changed way of handling files in Moodle 2.0, **Site files** as we know them no longer exist and in a new installation of Moodle 2.0 the link is absent. However, in a Moodle that has been upgraded to Moodle 2.0 you'll find a link called **Legacy site Files** where your original site files will be stored.

 Note that if we are actually working on the front page and have appropriate permissions, we also have a section in our **Settings** block to quickly access these front page settings. We saw this at the start of the chapter when looking at different users' views of the Navigation block.

What's new in server

As we saw at the start of the book, for Moodle 2.0 to function we require as a minimum:

- MySQL version 5.0.25 (contrasted with 4.1.6 in Moodle 1.9.8)
- PHP version 2.8 (contrasted with 4.3.0 in Moodle 1.9.8)

What's new in networking

If networking is enabled in **Advanced Features** we get a menu with networking settings and options similar to previous versions of Moodle. However what's new here is the ability to configure the profile fields to export and import over MNET when user accounts are created or updated. It's possible to override this for each MNET peer individually.

 Note that the following fields are compulsory: **username**, **email**, **firstname**, **lastname**, **auth**, **wwwroot**, **session.gc_lifetime**

What's new in reports

Let's move on to the really useful **Reports** link now.

Comments

As an administrator we have the right to see and delete any comments made throughout our Moodle site. We can view and edit them on the screen as in the following screenshot:

	author	content	action
	Emma Anforth	This course is set out in a very structured way. I like that	Delete
	Stuart Gorse	I think a structured approach is vital when learning a new language	Delete
	Andy Field	The course might benefit from a few more optional activities though, rather than all in linear progression	Delete
	Emma Anforth	That might be valuable later on but in the early stages I just want my hand held	Delete
	Stuart Gorse	Excellent. It's good to start with a positive foundation. Why not blog in French next time?	Delete
	Emma Anforth	C'est si difficile :(	Delete

Comments

Config changes

This screen gives us an at-a-glance view at changes made to the basic configuration of our Moodle site. This is particularly useful for problem tracking when multiple administrators are on a system or an external support provider has to track down an issue. In the next screenshot for instance, we see that anonymous feedback, portfolios, and RSS feeds had recently been enabled.

Config changes

Page: 1 2 3 4 5 6 7 8 9 10 11 12 13 14 15 16 17 18 ...23 (Next)

Date ↑	First name / Surname	Plugin	Setting	New value	Original value
Thursday, 5 August 2010, 04:57 PM	Moodle Fairy	core	feedback_allowfullanonymous	1	0
Thursday, 5 August 2010, 06:47 AM	Moodle Fairy	core	enableportfolios	1	0
Thursday, 5 August 2010, 06:47 AM	Moodle Fairy	core	enablerssfeeds	1	0

Question instances

Whereas in Moodle 1.9 we had a **Question** screen which reports on possible problems in our question database, in Moodle 2.0 we have a **Question instances** screen which will provide us with a list of all contexts in the system where there are questions of a particular type. Here's a report on instances of the True/False question type for example:

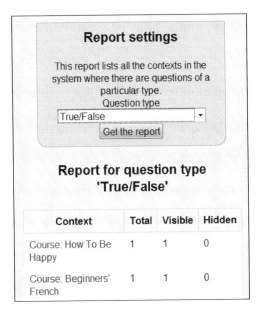

Development

Rather than calling itself **Miscellaneous** Moodle 2.0 has a **Development** section with the following items:

Experimental

Changes relating to groups and groupings are here:

- There is no longer an option to **enable groupings**; they are enabled by default
- There is an option to enable **the group members only** feature.

We can also transfer or export the contents of our Moodle database to another server.

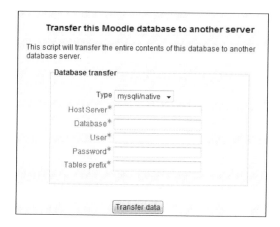

Web service test client

This is where we can test web service functions.

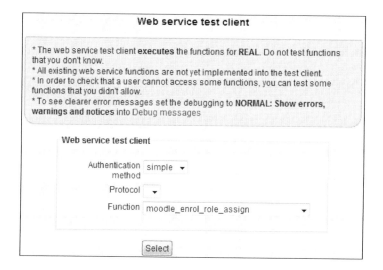

Purge all caches

Moodle can cache themes, JavaScript, language strings, filtered text, RSS feeds, and many other pieces of calculated data. Purging these caches will delete that data from the server and force browsers to refetch data, so that you can be sure you are seeing the most up-to-date values produced by the current code.

Moodle network test client

Our list of networked hosts, should we have some, will appear here.

Functional database tests

We can run functional database tests from here, choosing to show passes as well as fails.

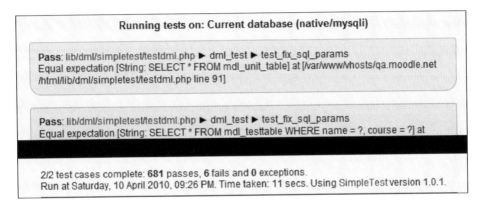

Running tests on: Current database (native/mysqli)

Pass: lib/dml/simpletest/testdml.php ▶ dml_test ▶ test_fix_sql_params
Equal expectation [String: SELECT * FROM mdl_unit_table] at [/var/www/vhosts/qa.moodle.net/html/lib/dml/simpletest/testdml.php line 91]

Pass: lib/dml/simpletest/testdml.php ▶ dml_test ▶ test_fix_sql_params
Equal expectation [String: SELECT * FROM mdl_testtable WHERE name = ?, course = ?] at

2/2 test cases complete: **681** passes, 6 fails and 0 exceptions.
Run at Saturday, 10 April 2010, 09:26 PM. Time taken: 11 secs. Using SimpleTest version 1.0.1.

Changes in Course administration

What a tutor sees in their **Settings** block depends on what has been enabled by admin. For instance, in the following screenshot our teacher Andy has the **Completion tracking** link below as he set up course completion in *Chapter 6, Managing the Learning Path*.

Some of these features we're familiar with already from earlier chapters; others we'll go through now.

How to enrol students into a course—the Users link

The **Users** link expands to the following:

- **Enrolled users** is where Andy or other tutors can see who is already on the course and where they can manually enrol others. If we look at what he sees when he accesses this link, we note, it tells us the role a user has, any groups they might be in, and how and when they were enrolled.

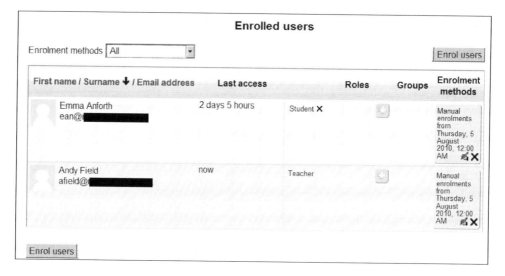

Note that, Andy can remove a role by clicking on the **X** and can add a role by clicking on the icon as shown in the following screenshot:

To enrol a new user he selects the **Enrol users** button and a list appears of the available users for him to choose from. He's also given the option to specify their role, enrolment date, and duration. He enrolls the user by clicking on the **Enrol** button.

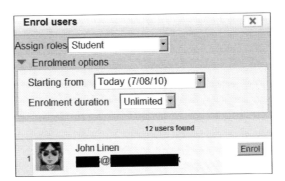

A user with category capabilities such as our Moodle manager Martin would have an extra button, **Enrol cohort**, which he could click on to bring in a selected cohort to the course, (in this instance, ten students from the **Autumn Intake** cohort.) This, of course, is assuming the Cohort sync plugin has been enabled in enrolment methods.

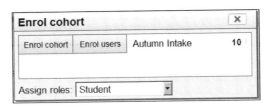

- **Enrolment methods**: This is where a teacher can add, edit, or delete enrolment methods for a particular course. What they can add depends on what has been enabled by admin and their own permissions. For instance, Martin was able previously to add the Cohort sync and therefore, enrol a cohort. Teacher Andy's view is shown in the following screenshot:

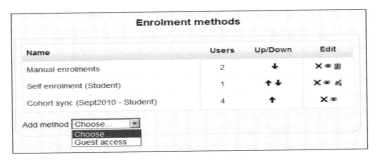

One of these is **Self enrolment (Student)**. As this is enabled, it has a link in **Course Administration** which opens up to the following screen:

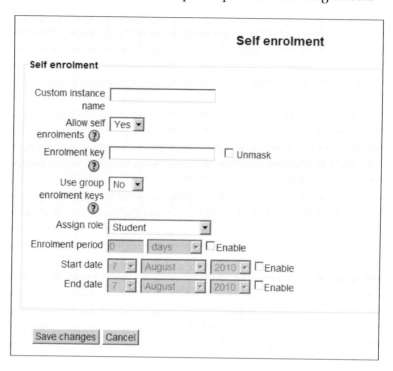

- **Groups**: Here's where Andy can create groups and set group enrolment keys for students when they self-enrol, as allowed in the settings we explored just now

- **Permissions**: As seen before, Andy can check permissions relating to enrolment here

- **Other Users**: This link displays users like our Moodle manager Martin who aren't actually enrolled in the course but do have roles associated with it.

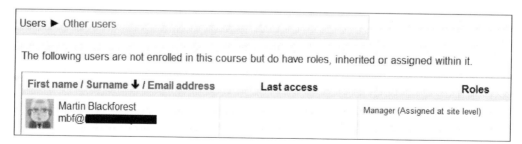

How to back up a course—the Backup link

As with later versions of Moodle 1.9, regular teachers can't include user information in their course backup. Compare teacher Andy's locked down view (right) when clicking **Backup** with an admin's or Manager's (left).

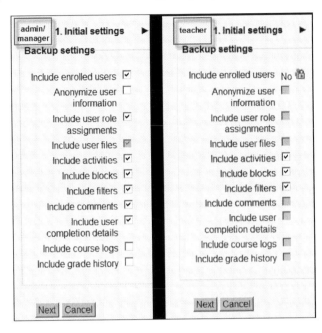

As Moodle 2.0 offers more features, the backup options are increased. For example:

- Do we want to include comments?
- Do we want to include user completion details?
- Do we want to include the dedicated course filter settings?

Having made our choices, we are then taken through the following sequence:

1. **Initial settings**: These are as in the previous screenshot.

2. **Schema settings**: Where we choose which items to include and whether to include user information. Note how teacher Andy's would be restricted:

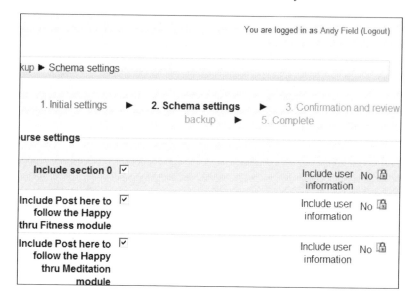

3. **Confirmation and review**: Where we can rename the zipped file and check we have added everything we want.

4. **Perform backup**: This sets the backup in motion.

5. **Complete**: Our course has now been backed up. The following screenshot shows an example of a **Front Page** backup:

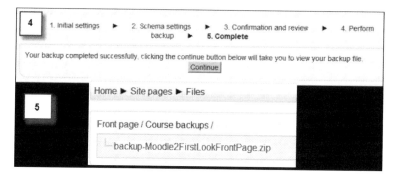

How to restore a course—the Restore link

Our teacher on the *Beginners' French* course, Stuart, would like to restore to our Moodle 2.0 a course *Intermediate French* that he used elsewhere. Let's follow his steps:

1. He uses a new, empty course that's been set up for him and clicks **Restore** in **Course Administration**.

2. He is then taken to a screen where he can choose from already backed up files or upload a previously backed up course:

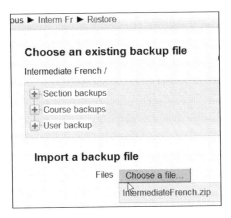

3. Stuart clicks on **Restore** at the bottom of the screen.

4. Following this, a similar path appears to when Andy backed up his course. Stuart follows this, making appropriate choices until his course is restored.

How to share a course – the Publish link

If the Moodle admin has enabled the Community Hub then clicking here will allow a teacher to share their course:

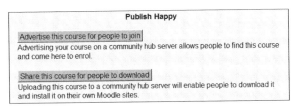

Repositories

If a teacher has been allowed to add their own repository instances to their course they may do so here. They can also see which repositories are available.

Where are the course files?

Our teacher Andy has a link **Legacy course files**. This is only here because he upgraded from Moodle 1.9. He doesn't use it for uploading into. A brand new course on Moodle 2.0 wouldn't have a **Course files** link at all, as we have previously discovered.

Summary

In this chapter, we've taken a brief journey through the administration features of Moodle 2.0, both from an admin and then a course tutor's point of view. We've focused on what's new and what's different from Moodle 1.9.

If we had to pick out the salient features in a few bullet points we might select:

- Increased efficiency and clarity of roles.
- Improved interaction with the Open Web—both going out of Moodle and coming in.
- Better management of enrolments.
- Enhanced appearance—both navigationally and thematically.

At the time of writing, Moodle 2.0 was in preview mode (beta).At the time of publication it will be on Candidate Release 1. Things change fast, the world changes fast, and Moodle 2.0 is changing with it. If you find some features different in your install from here, do let Packt know and we'll adapt the relevant sections of the book in the next revision. If there are some features missing that you'd hoped were coming, be patient. While we're still awaiting the release of Moodle 2.0, developers at a meeting at the end of 2009 started planning for Moodle 3.0 It will be upon us sooner than we think!

Index

W

Webdav repository 67
Wiki module 13, 14, 96, 106, 107, 108
WordPress 50
workshop
  features 113
Workshop module 13
  about 96, 112
  assessment phase 121-123
  gradebook 127
  grading evaluation phase 123-126
  set-up phase 113
  submission phase 117-120
WYSIWYG 49

Y

YouTube
  URL 12

Made in the USA
Lexington, KY
18 April 2013